OCEAN ANATOMY
ACTIVITIES FOR KIDS

Fun, Hands-On Learning

BY LAURA PETRUSIC

ILLUSTRATED BY KIM MALEK

ROCKRIDGE
PRESS

Copyright © 2021 by Rockridge Press, Emeryville, California

No part of this publication may be reproduced, stored in a retrieval system, or transmitted in any form or by any means, electronic, mechanical, photocopying, recording, scanning, or otherwise, except as permitted under Sections 107 or 108 of the 1976 United States Copyright Act, without the prior written permission of the Publisher. Requests to the Publisher for permission should be addressed to the Permissions Department, Rockridge Press, 6005 Shellmound Street, Suite 175, Emeryville, CA 94608.

Limit of Liability/Disclaimer of Warranty: The Publisher and the author make no representations or warranties with respect to the accuracy or completeness of the contents of this work and specifically disclaim all warranties, including without limitation warranties of fitness for a particular purpose. No warranty may be created or extended by sales or promotional materials. The advice and strategies contained herein may not be suitable for every situation. This work is sold with the understanding that the Publisher is not engaged in rendering medical, legal, or other professional advice or services. If professional assistance is required, the services of a competent professional person should be sought. Neither the Publisher nor the author shall be liable for damages arising herefrom. The fact that an individual, organization, or website is referred to in this work as a citation and/or potential source of further information does not mean that the author or the Publisher endorses the information the individual, organization, or website may provide or recommendations they/it may make. Further, readers should be aware that websites listed in this work may have changed or disappeared between when this work was written and when it is read.

For general information on our other products and services or to obtain technical support, please contact our Customer Care Department within the United States at (866) 744-2665, or outside the United States at (510) 253-0500.

Rockridge Press publishes its books in a variety of electronic and print formats. Some content that appears in print may not be available in electronic books, and vice versa.

TRADEMARKS: Rockridge Press and the Rockridge Press logo are trademarks or registered trademarks of Callisto Media Inc. and/or its affiliates, in the United States and other countries, and may not be used without written permission. All other trademarks are the property of their respective owners. Rockridge Press is not associated with any product or vendor mentioned in this book.

Series Designers: Jane Archer and Karmen Lizzul
Interior and Cover Designer: Jennifer Hsu
Art Producer: Tom Hood
Editor: Laura Apperson
Production Editor: Jenna Dutton
Production Manager: Riley Hoffman

Illustrations © Kim Malek 2021. Author photograph courtesy of Chella Photography.

ISBN: Print 978-1-64876-324-3 | eBook 978-1-64876-325-0
R0

FOR MY CHILDREN,
ADAM, MEGAN, AND BEN—
MY FAVORITE MARINE
SCIENCE EXPLORERS.

CONTENTS

DIVE INTO THE DEEP BLUE SEA — vi

1: THE ANATOMY OF THE OCEAN — 1

2: FISH AND MARINE MAMMALS — 19

3: COASTS AND SHORELINES — 37

4: CORAL REEFS — 51

5: DEEP SEA — 65

6: POLAR REGIONS — 79

RESOURCES — 93

DIVE INTO THE DEEP BLUE SEA

Welcome, future marine scientist! In this book, you will get to act like an explorer and think like a scientist as you learn about the anatomy of the ocean. Ocean explorers and marine scientists follow five basic steps to study the natural world around them. Following these steps provides validity and reliability to their discoveries. Let's explore how scientists have used these skills to learn more about the ocean.

The first step is to **observe**. Marine scientists, like Eugenie Clark, observe what they are studying. Clark was an American ichthyologist, or fish scientist, specializing in shark research. She and her colleagues noticed that sharks avoided a fish called the Moses sole. Her subsequent studies showed that this fish created an effective natural form of shark repellant.

The second step is to **ask** questions. For example, Sylvia Earle, an American oceanographer, wanted to answer the question *What diversity of marine life lies at the bottom of the ocean?* To answer this question, she founded Deep Ocean Engineering, a company that designed a state-of-the-art research submarine that allowed researchers to collect important data about the deep-sea environment.

The third step is to **imagine**. Charles Darwin, a naturalist and geologist famous for his theory of evolution, spent a lot of time documenting organisms in various habitats. His study of marine life focused on coral reef growth. He observed that coral reefs grew upward from deep reef structures around islands. He imagined the land surrounding the reef as slowly sinking over time while the reef continued to grow up toward the surface. This would explain how coral reef *atolls*, or reefs that surround a lagoon, formed from ancient sea volcanoes.

The fourth step is to **test**. Jacques-Yves Cousteau was a French naval officer, filmmaker, author, and researcher. Cousteau and Emile Gagnan, a French engineer, developed the first self-contained underwater breathing apparatus (*scuba*): the Aqua-Lung. Then, Hans Hass, an Austrian marine biologist, redesigned and tested different versions of the Aqua-Lung in order to create the advanced scuba equipment used by divers today.

The fifth step is to **reflect** on the results and ask how the information is important. For example, Rachel Carson, an American biologist, reviewed reports on fish populations for the US Fish and Wildlife Service. By reflecting on her research findings, she was able to write educational articles for the public on the health of the environment and its potential impact on humans.

In completing the lessons and activities in this book, you will build the same skills used by famous ocean explorers and marine scientists: *observing*, *asking*, *imagining*, *testing*, and *reflecting*. These five skills are useful to anyone who studies the natural world.

HOW TO USE THIS BOOK

This book is designed to be easy to navigate. Each of the six chapters explores a topic related to the world's oceans: anatomy of an ocean, fish and marine mammals, coasts and shorelines, coral reefs, the deep sea, and the polar regions. Each chapter contains three to four lessons along with an activity to inspire you to ask questions about the ocean and the life within it. You will be able to imagine the effects of natural ocean systems and test *hypotheses*, or ideas. Reflecting on these activities will help you better understand our ocean world. Let's dive in to see how each chapter is organized.

THE LESSON

There are 20 lessons divided among the six chapters. Each lesson gives you a learning *objective*, or goal. For example, in chapter 1, the lesson about ocean zones helps you understand how sunlight filtration changes with ocean depth. Each lesson asks you to imagine something in the natural world and consider the answers to thought-provoking questions. These questions prepare you for the activity, where you will test what you have learned and write down key observations in your journal, just like a scientist.

THE ACTIVITY

Activities come right after the lessons. Each activity begins with a summary of the learning objective, followed by a list of materials and prep work you'll need to do before starting the activity. Step-by-step instructions will guide you to create, model, simulate, or experiment. Some activities may require extra caution. Adult supervision for activities are indicated with a **Safety First!** warning. You'll also find a section that includes tips and ideas for even more activities.

OCEAN JOURNAL ENTRY

In addition to this book, you're going to need a blank journal where you can write down your ideas, questions, experiment methods, and observations. As you read the lessons and complete the activities, you might draw some data tables, make some drawings, write observations, or make hypotheses.

Most important, your journal is the place for you to reflect on what you've learned and answer the questions in each lesson. There will also be journal prompts after each activity—this is your place to write your thoughts.

What type of journal you use is completely up to you. Just pick out something you like and that inspires you. How you organize it is also your decision. You might want to divide your journal into 20 sections, one for each lesson and activity. Then, you can create subheadings such as "Questions," "Observations," "Hypotheses," and "Journal Prompts." You could also create entries in order with specific dates and headings, such as "Ocean Zones: Journal Prompts." Do what works for you.

Now that you've learned how to use this book, it's time to take the plunge and explore the anatomy of the ocean!

DIVE INTO THE DEEP BLUE SEA

THE ANATOMY OF THE OCEAN

The enormous body of saltwater we call the ocean covers 71 percent of the Earth's surface. While our world's oceans are connected, they are divided into five different basins: the Atlantic, the Pacific, the Indian, the Arctic, and the Southern Ocean (Antarctic).

Have you ever wondered what they are made of? Or how deep they are? Or what causes the waves that endlessly crash on the shore? In this chapter, you will dive into the deepest parts of the ocean to learn how it changes from top to bottom, observe how and what moves ocean waters, and explore why the ocean is salty.

LESSON

OCEAN ZONES

The ocean has five *zones*, or layers: sunlight, or *epipelagic*; twilight, or *mesopelagic*; midnight, or *bathypelagic*; abyss, or *abyssalpelagic*; and the hadal zone, or *hadalpelagic*. Each layer begins at a specific depth below the ocean surface. Light at the surface is quickly filtered out. In fact, no sunlight reaches below 3,280 feet (1,000 m) in the ocean. This leaves most of the ocean cold and dark. Let's explore each layer in more detail.

Sunlight Zone: The sunlight zone, or epipelagic layer, starts at the surface of the ocean and goes down 656 feet (200 m). Most of the organisms of the ocean live in this zone because enough light can penetrate for photosynthesis to take place. *Photosynthesis* is the chemical process that *phytoplankton*, microscopic single-celled, plantlike organisms, use to make energy. There are 5,000 known species of phytoplankton alone, and scientists estimate they make 50 to 85 percent of the world's oxygen from their photosynthesis. The other type of plankton are *zooplankton*, animallike single-celled organisms that feed on phytoplankton. These species form the base of the food chain in most ocean ecosystems.

Twilight Zone: The twilight zone, or mesopelagic layer, begins at a depth of 656 feet (200 m) and goes down to 3,280 feet (1,000 m). The last bit of surface light reaches this layer, but not enough for photosynthesis. Without the sun's energy to warm these waters, temperatures drop quickly. The top of the twilight zone can have temperatures around 70 degrees Fahrenheit (21°C), but the deeper it gets, the temperature quickly drops to about 40 degrees Fahrenheit (4°C).

Midnight Zone: The third layer—the midnight zone, or bathylpelagic—begins just below the twilight zone and reaches a depth of just over 13,000 feet (4,000 m) below sea level, or below the surface of the ocean. The only light in this zone comes from *bioluminescence* created by the creatures living here, meaning they can glow from within. In the ocean, bioluminescence can be seen in animals such as the deep-sea angler fish, which looks like it has a fishing lure attached to its head that glows blue to attract prey (page 76).

LESSON

Abyssal Zone: The fourth layer, also called the abyssalpelagic zone, reaches down past the midnight zone to almost 20,000 feet (6,000 m) below the surface. Only a few creatures can be found at these depths. One example is a sea pig. A sea pig is not really a pig, but a sea cucumber—an *invertebrate*, or organism without a skeleton, related to sea stars. Sea pigs use their branching tentacles to eat decaying material on the seafloor. Because their skin is poisonous, they have very few predators.

Hadal Zone: The last and deepest layer of the ocean goes down into deep trenches that extend below the seafloor. One of the most abundant organisms at these depths is the amphipod, a soft-shelled crustacean that looks like a flea. As scavengers, they search the trenches for decaying organisms for food.

Fun Fact

The lowest point on Earth is Challenger Deep in the Mariana Trench, at a depth of 35,827 feet (almost 7 miles). You would need to stack more than 1,020 school buses from front to back to reach the bottom!

THE ANATOMY OF THE OCEAN   3

ACTIVITY

LAYERS OF LIGHT

TIME: 20 TO 30 MINUTES

CATEGORY: INDOOR, MODEL

MATERIALS

PENCIL AND STICKY NOTES (OR PAPER) FOR LABELING

MEASURING CUPS

3 (8-OUNCE) CLEAR PLASTIC CUPS

WATER

RED, BLUE, AND GREEN FOOD COLORING

SPOON, FOR MIXING

1/8 CUP OF WASHABLE BLACK PAINT

FLASHLIGHT

TIP:

→ Wash the spoon in between mixing each cup. This will avoid transferring materials from one "zone" to the next.

What would we be able to see at the bottom of the ocean? Would you need to use a flashlight? In this activity, you will create a model of how light filters through the five layers of the ocean.

PREP WORK

1. Gather all the materials into a place you don't mind getting wet.

2. Label 1 sticky note for each of the following: sunlight, twilight, deep-sea zones (grouping the midnight, abyssal, and hadal zones together).

3. Use the measuring cup to fill each plastic cup with ¾ cup of water.

STEP-BY-STEP INSTRUCTIONS

1. First, create the top layer, the sunlight zone. In one of the prepared plastic cups filled with water, add 1 drop of green food coloring. Gently stir with the spoon until the food coloring is completely mixed. Place the *sunlight* label directly under this cup, with the word facing up, covering the written part of the label completely.

2. Next, add 10 drops of blue food coloring into another prepared cup with water, stirring to mix. Place the *twilight* label under this cup, with the word facing up.

3. The last prepared cup will represent the darkest parts of the ocean, the deep sea. Pour the black paint in the water, stirring to mix completely. Add 5 drops of red food coloring and stir to mix completely. Place the *deep-sea zones* label under this cup, with the words facing up.

OCEAN ANATOMY ACTIVITIES FOR KIDS

4. Observe your cups from the surface. How many labels are you able to read through the top of the water?

5. Place a flashlight on one side of each cup. Observe how much light shines through to the other side. Which zone allows the most light through the cup? Which zone(s) allow the least?

CONCLUSION:
Light is filtered from the layers of ocean water as you descend below the surface. In the deepest parts of the ocean, light can't get through. By observing how the flashlight filters through each cup, you were able to observe how each of these areas of the ocean filter light.

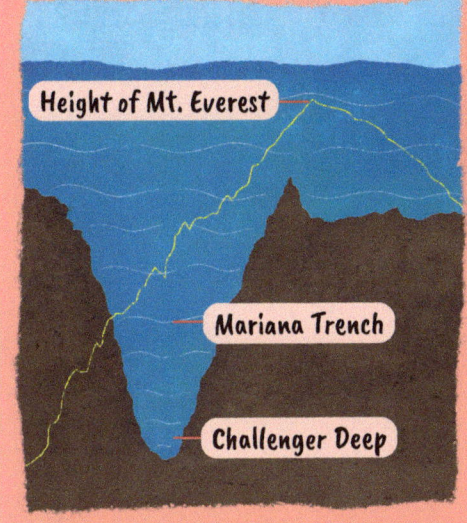

OCEAN JOURNAL ENTRY

Now that you have explored how the ocean changes from top to bottom, let's reflect on how those changes affect life in the ocean. Write the answers to the following questions in your journal.

1. *Photosynthesis cannot occur past the sunlight zone. Where do you think animals in deep waters get their energy?*

2. *Since there is no light in the deepest parts of the ocean, how do animals living there know where they are and where they are going?*

THE ANATOMY OF THE OCEAN   5

LESSON

WHY IS THE OCEAN SALTY?

The *salinity*, or how salty something is, of seawater is 35 parts per thousand. That means that if all the salt was taken out of 1,000 buckets of seawater, there would be 35 buckets filled with just salt! If you have ever gone swimming in the ocean, you may have noticed that as you dry off, a layer of salt remains on your skin and hair. When the saltwater from the ocean evaporates, the salt that was dissolved in the ocean water is left behind. It's too heavy to form a gas with the water, so it stays on your skin instead.

To understand where all the salt in the ocean comes from, it's important to learn about the minerals in Earth's *crust*, or the outside layer of the Earth. The crust of the Earth is made up of many different rocks and minerals. One of these minerals is salt. A combination of elements in the water—including sodium, chlorine, magnesium, calcium, potassium, and bromine—form different kinds of mineral salts. The most common salt in the ocean is made of the elements sodium and chlorine, which forms sodium chloride. This is also the same type of salt we use to season our food.

Fun Fact

Many animals that live in the ocean have adaptations to remove the salt from the water they consume. For example, sea turtles get rid of salt through their "tears!"

LESSON

Thanks to the *water cycle*, the minerals found in the Earth's crust are redistributed into the oceans. Freshwater *precipitation*, like rain or snow, pours over the land and flows into rivers and streams. Along the way, it dissolves the salt in the ground. Eventually, these lakes and streams make their way into the ocean, taking the salt with it. As the ocean water evaporates, it creates clouds, and the salt from the Earth's crust is left behind in the ocean, making it salty. Many of these rain clouds travel to the land and repeat again the process of dissolving salt and bringing it to the ocean.

ACTIVITY

DISSOLVING THE EARTH'S CRUST

TIME:
15 TO 20 MINUTES

CATEGORY:
INDOOR, MODEL

MATERIALS
CLEAR OR WHITE SHALLOW DISH

ROOM TEMPERATURE WATER

SEVERAL ROUND, RED-AND-WHITE-STRIPED PEPPERMINT CANDIES

HOT TAP WATER

SPOON

Where does the ocean's salt come from? In this activity you will model the process of salt dissolving from the Earth's crust, and you will explore the factors that affect the amount of salt that can dissolve in water.

PREP WORK

1. Gather your materials to work in an area you don't mind getting wet.

2. Fill the dish with ½ inch of room temperature water—just enough to cover the bottom of the dish.

Safety First! *Be very careful when working with hot water to avoid burns.*

STEP-BY-STEP INSTRUCTIONS

1. Gently place one peppermint candy, flat-side down, in the dish. Imagine that the peppermint is the Earth's crust.

2. Allow your peppermint to sit in the water untouched for 1 minute. The peppermint is like a piece of the Earth's crust sitting under a lake or stream. What do you think will happen to the peppermint?

3. After the resting time is over, observe what happened to the peppermint. Record your observations in your journal.

4. Gently slide the peppermint across the bottom of the dish. What do you notice? What happened to the red coloring of the peppermint?

TIP:

➡ If you are having trouble seeing the red peppermint dye in a clear dish, try placing a white piece of paper under your dish.

OCEAN ANATOMY ACTIVITIES FOR KIDS

5. Repeat the experiment using hot tap water. Use a spoon to move the peppermint in the water so you don't burn your hands. What happens to the peppermint? How is this the same or different from your first experiment? Record your observation in your journal.

CONCLUSION:
You have just observed the sugar of a solid peppermint candy dissolve in freshwater, similar to the way rainwater dissolves salt from the Earth's crust. Water seeping into the Earth's crust and flowing into rivers or streams dissolves the salt and eventually carries it to the ocean. Salt then builds up in the ocean as seawater evaporates to form clouds, beginning the process all over again.

OCEAN JOURNAL ENTRY

In this activity you simulated the creation of salty seawater. Consider your observations from this activity to help you answer the following questions in your journal.

1. *What do you think would happen if you left the peppermint in the water for a few days?*

2. *Do you think there is a limit to how much salt the ocean can hold? Explain why or why not.*

THE ANATOMY OF THE OCEAN   9

LESSON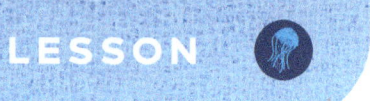

OCEAN CURRENTS

The crashing of waves at the beach is one way we experience the constant motion of the ocean. In this lesson we will learn where and how the ocean moves, as well as the forces that create this motion.

The movement of ocean water from one location to another is called a *current*. Surface currents are usually caused by wind, though the gravitational pull of the Sun and Moon also play a factor. The strength of wind-driven surface currents depends on the direction, speed, and duration (or time) the wind blows against the surface of the ocean. We experience these surface currents as waves. Waves are energy moving through water toward the shore. The longer, faster, and larger the *fetch*, or the ocean surface area affected, the greater the movement of the water.

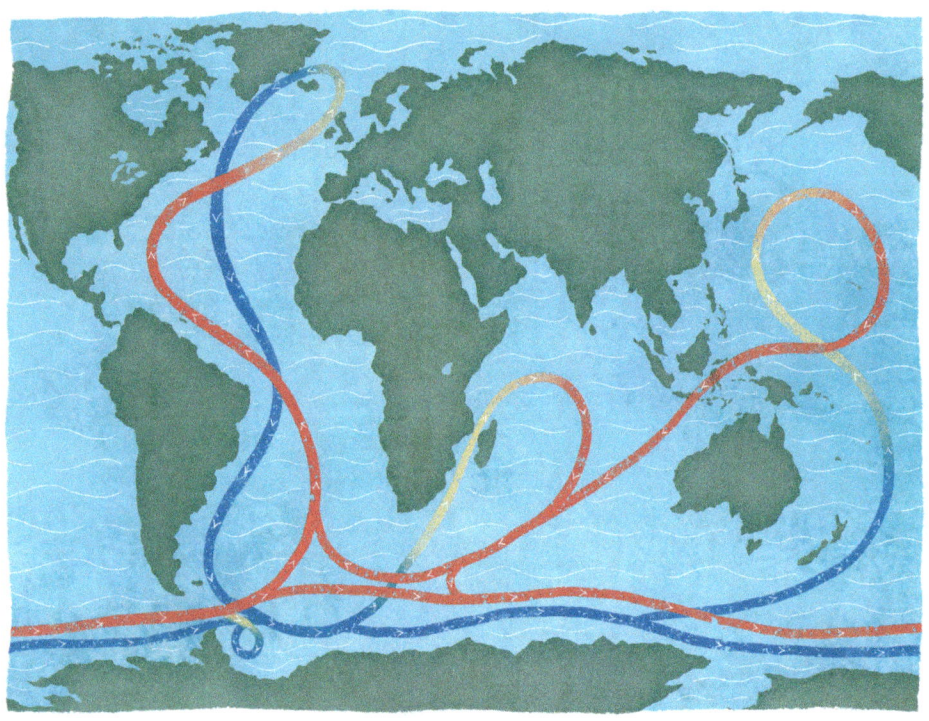

 COLD WATER    HOT WATER

10   OCEAN ANATOMY ACTIVITIES FOR KIDS

LESSON

Deep ocean currents are formed by a few more factors, which include the temperature and salinity of the water. Cold salty water tends to sink below warmer freshwater. This sinking creates a slow movement of water from high latitudes near the North and South poles toward the warmer waters near the equator.

The rotation of the Earth also affects the flow of currents. It moves the currents in a circular pattern called the *Coriolis effect*. Because of this effect, currents within each ocean basin move in a clockwise direction toward the North Pole in the northern hemisphere, and, in the southern hemisphere, a counterclockwise direction toward the South Pole. Ocean basins are large, bowl-shaped areas of the Earth that hold the major oceans. At the equator, these surface currents separate and draw cold water from deep currents coming from the poles, warming it at the surface. Surface and deep-water currents carry water all around the globe in a cycle called the *global ocean conveyor belt*. This conveyor belt continuously carries deep, cold water from the North and South poles to the equator and warm surface waters from the equator back to the poles.

Fun Fact

It takes approximately 1,000 years for one drop of water to circle the globe on the global ocean conveyor belt.

ACTIVITY

CREATING CURRENTS

TIME:
15 TO 20 MINUTES

CATEGORY:
INDOOR, EXPERIMENT

MATERIALS
ROCKS AND GRAVEL
9-BY-13-INCH SHALLOW METAL PAN
ROOM TEMPERATURE WATER
GROUND BLACK PEPPER
DRINKING STRAW

TIP:
➤ If you can't tell which direction the black pepper is traveling, try adding more pepper, a little at a time, until you notice a pattern forming on the surface of the water.

In this activity you will observe the effect *landforms* (or features of the Earth), wind direction, and wind duration have on floating materials on the surface of the ocean. You will create a model of an ocean basin and observe how changes made to this model affect how water moves through the basin.

PREP WORK

1. Gather your materials to work in a place you don't mind getting wet.

2. Arrange the rocks and gravel into piles at the edges of the pan, leaving space in the middle. These represent landforms.

3. Fill the pan with water, leaving the top of some of your "landforms" out of the water. This creates a model of an ocean basin.

STEP-BY-STEP INSTRUCTIONS

1. Shake a small amount of black pepper onto the surface of the water. Imagine that this is debris floating on the surface of the ocean.

2. Without touching the surface, blow gently through the straw from one side of the pan. This represents wind blowing over an ocean basin. What happens to the pepper on the surface?

3. Stop blowing through the straw and observe the location of the pepper. How did it change?

4. Begin blowing gently again through the straw in a different area over the pan. How does the position of the pepper change? How is it the same?

5. Repeat the experiment, changing the position and shape of the rocks and gravel. What changed? What stayed the same?

CONCLUSION:

You have just created surface currents in a model of an ocean basin. How long, how fast, and from what direction the wind interacts with the surface of the ocean are major factors that determine these ocean currents. The longer you blow in a particular direction, the faster water in the model circles in the basin. The shape of the rocks and gravel, representing landforms, can also change the speed and directions of these currents.

OCEAN JOURNAL ENTRY

In this lesson you observed the effect that wind has in creating currents across the surface of the ocean. Use your experience from this activity to answer the following questions in your journal.

1. *What effect does wind have on debris gathering on the surface of the ocean?*

2. *If you were to blow over the pan without a straw, what factor would be changing: the speed, direction, area, or duration of wind blowing on the ocean surface?*

3. *Describe some ways you think currents affect marine life.*

THE ANATOMY OF THE OCEAN

LESSON

TIDES

When we jump up in the air, the Earth's gravity brings us back down to the ground. *Gravity* is the invisible force created by the Earth that pulls objects toward its surface. The Earth's gravity is so strong that it keeps all of the ocean's water from flowing out into space. Like the Earth, the Moon and the Sun also have gravity. In fact, gravity keeps the Earth in orbit around the Sun, and the Moon in orbit around the Earth.

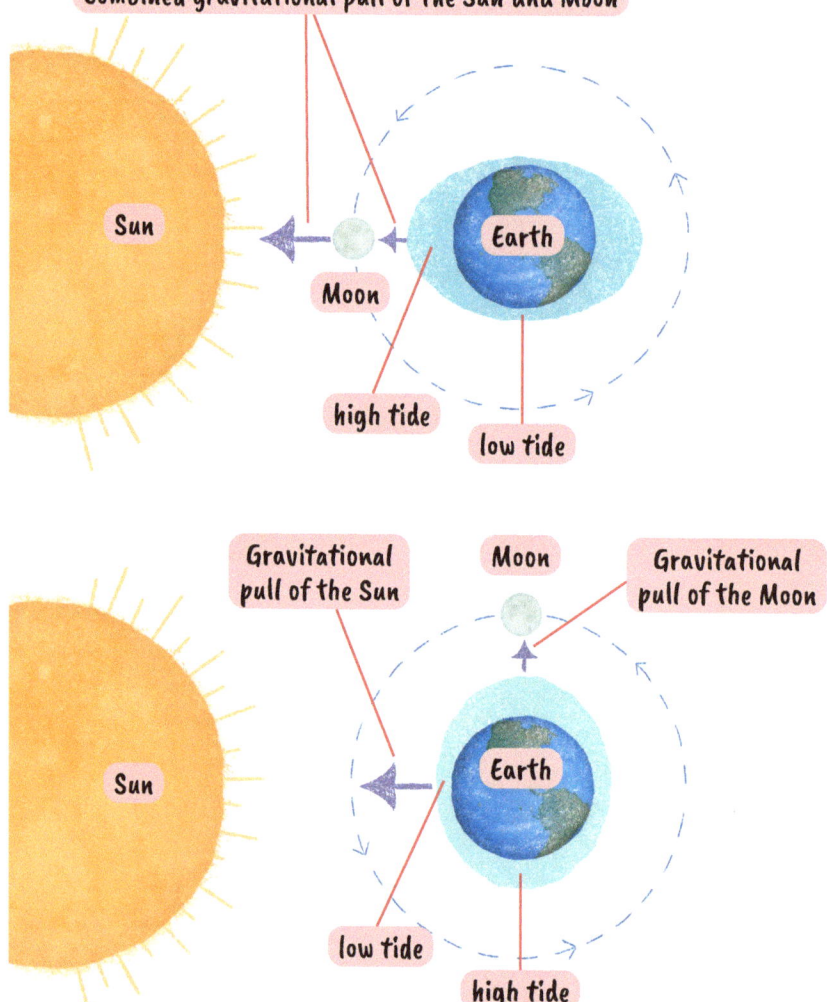

14   OCEAN ANATOMY ACTIVITIES FOR KIDS

LESSON

The changing gravitational pull of the Sun and Moon can be observed in the ocean as *tides*, or the periodic rise and fall of sea level. The gravity from the Sun and Moon cause the sea level to bulge. That bulge follows the Moon and Sun around the globe. The positions of the Sun, Moon, and Earth change in daily, monthly, and yearly cycles. Because we can predict these positions in relationship to one another, we can also predict the position of tides as they change.

The daily rise and fall of the tides is called a *tidal cycle*. Some areas of the globe can experience as many as two high and low tides a day. When the sea level rises to its highest point, it's called *high tide*. When it falls to its lowest point, it's called *low tide*. The *tidal range* is the change in height of sea level from low and high tide. During a full moon and a new moon, tidal ranges are at their greatest, meaning that coastlines will experience the highest high tide and the lowest low tide during those times.

Fun Fact

The Bay of Fundy in Canada is considered to have the largest tidal range in the world. The sea level there can rise and fall up to 53 feet (16.15 m) in just one day!

THE ANATOMY OF THE OCEAN **15**

ACTIVITY

MOVING WATER WITH THE MOON

TIME:
15 TO 20 MINUTES

CATEGORY:
INDOOR, SIMULATION

MATERIALS
20 PAPER CLIPS
EMPTY PLASTIC WATER BOTTLE
2 LARGE MAGNETS (AT LEAST ½ CM THICK AND 2 CM LONG)

How does the Moon's gravity affect the ocean's sea level? How and why do the tides move? In this activity you will create a simulation of how the Moon's gravitational pull raises sea level and how it travels around the globe.

PREP WORK

Put the paper clips inside the plastic bottle and seal the bottle.

STEP-BY-STEP INSTRUCTIONS

1. Imagine that the paper clips in the bottle are the ocean's waters attached to the Earth and that the magnet is the Moon. Place one magnet up against the side of the water bottle near the top of the paper clip pile. What happens to the paper clips? How is this like the gravitational pull of the Moon on the waters of the Earth?

2. Move the magnet around the outside of the water bottle. This simulates the rotation of the Moon around the Earth. What happens to the paper clips? Record your observations in your journal.

3. Try placing the other magnet on the opposite side of the water bottle from the Moon. This represents the effect of the Sun's gravitational pull on the ocean. What do you notice? Record your observations in your journal.

TIPS:

➡ Hold your bottle upright when moving the magnet.

➡ Experiment with different-sized magnets to achieve a stronger hold on the paper clips within the bottle.

OCEAN ANATOMY ACTIVITIES FOR KIDS

CONCLUSION:

The paper clips in this activity were attracted to the magnet similar to how the ocean waters are pulled by the gravity of the Sun and the Moon. Because the position of the Earth changes constantly in relationship to the Sun and the Moon, sea level rises and falls periodically throughout the day. Because we can predict the positions of the Sun, Moon, and Earth, we can predict the tides throughout the Earth.

OCEAN JOURNAL ENTRY

In this activity you simulated the movement of tides around the globe due to the movement of the Moon and Sun in relationship to the Earth. Reflect on this activity to help you answer the following questions in your journal.

1. *Describe how the force of the magnet on the paper clips is like the gravitational pull of the Moon on the ocean.*

2. *Reflect on your observations when using two magnets to represent the Sun and the Moon. If both the Sun and the Moon have a gravitational pull on the Earth, do you think their forces can combine to create a larger tide? Why or why not?*

3. *Why might it be helpful to predict the change in tides in places like the Bay of Fundy?*

FISH AND MARINE MAMMALS

The more than two million species of marine life are connected to each other through a *food web*, a series of interconnected food chains sustaining life. Food chains are a transfer of energy from one organism to another beginning with *producers*, or organisms that create their own food, such as phytoplankton. These producers provide a food source for *consumers* that eat them, such as animals like coral or crustaceans.

In this chapter, you will explore how animals find their way in the ocean, capture their prey, and swim with ease. This chapter is all about the diversity of marine life and the adaptations they have evolved for survival in their watery world.

LESSON

ANATOMY OF A FISH

Fish are animals with unique adaptations for life in the ocean. Instead of using lungs to breathe like humans, fish use gills. When water is pumped over the gills, oxygen is collected and carbon dioxide is released. Some fish pump water over their gills with a bony plate called an *operculum*, or gill cover. Many fish swim in large groups called *schools*, which help keep them safe if a predator attacks. Most fish have fins to help them swim through the water.

Most fish species lay eggs and are *cold-blooded*, meaning they stay the same temperature as their surrounding environment. The fish species that do not lay eggs keep those eggs inside their bodies until they hatch. Male seahorses have a large pouch near their stomachs that hold their eggs until they are ready to hatch.

Most fish species are adapted to swimming upright, or vertically in the *water column*, the area between the seafloor and the surface in a specific spot. Some fish, like flounders, are flat-looking with mouths located under their bodies. This mouth position allows them to eat food on the seafloor as they swim over it. Flounders can also change their coloring to match the seafloor, disguising them from predators.

To understand more how fish are adapted to ocean life, let's explore why some objects float and some sink. *Buoyancy*, the upward force that water has on a submerged object, determines how well something floats. An object's buoyancy mostly depends on the object's density, not its size. Density is how much matter is in an object, or the *mass*, compared to how much space the object takes up, or the *volume*. For example, if you threw an orange and a penny into a swimming pool, the orange would float, but the penny would sink. Even though the orange is bigger than the penny, the penny is denser. It has more matter in a smaller space. If an object's density is lower than the density of water, like the orange, it will float. The penny's density is greater than water, so it sinks.

LESSON

Fish are usually denser than ocean water is, which makes them sink. To prevent this, many fish have a *swim bladder*. Swim bladders are gas-filled organs inside the fish that can be emptied or filled to control the fish's buoyancy. The fish is able to control how much gas is in the swim bladder as needed. More gas in the swim bladder increases the volume of the fish, making it *positively buoyant*, allowing the fish to float up to the surface. Letting out the gas decreases the fish's volume, making it *negatively buoyant*, and lets the fish sink to a depth it wants. A fish that neither sinks nor floats is described as *neutrally buoyant*.

How is neutral buoyancy helpful to fish? Imagine constantly treading water in the deep end of a swimming pool to stay at the surface. Over time you could become extremely tired! If a fish does not have a swim bladder, it must continue to use energy to keep swimming.

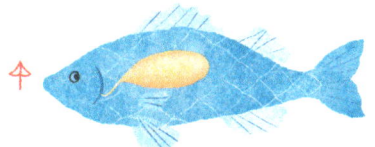
filled with oxygen

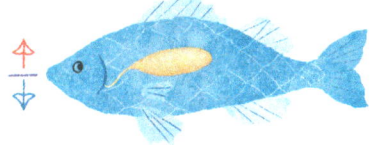
slightly deflated

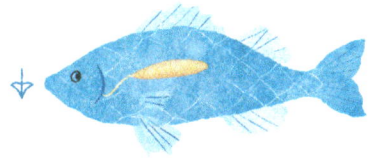
much less oxygen

Fun Fact

Sharks and stingrays don't have swim bladders. They control their buoyancy with oils in their liver. Oil is less dense than water, so it helps keep the shark from sinking.

FISH AND MARINE MAMMALS

ACTIVITY

FISH FLOATS

TIME:
10 TO 20 MINUTES

CATEGORY:
INDOOR, EXPERIMENT

MATERIALS
5-GALLON CLEAR PLASTIC CONTAINER

SEVERAL ROCKS SMALL ENOUGH TO FIT THROUGH THE OPENING OF THE PLASTIC BOTTLE

EMPTY 12-OUNCE PLASTIC WATER BOTTLE

How do fish stay afloat without sinking to the bottom of the ocean? In this activity, you will experiment with mass and volume to create neutral buoyancy, similar to the way fish create neutral buoyancy in their swim bladders.

PREP WORK

1. Gather your materials to work in an area you don't mind getting wet.

2. Fill the container with water up to 5 inches from the top.

STEP-BY-STEP INSTRUCTIONS

1. Imagine that the water bottle is a fish living in the middle of the water column—between the seafloor and the surface. The container is the fish's environment, or the ocean. The air space inside the bottle is the swim bladder of the fish. The stones are the mass of the fish.

2. Create a hypothesis by guessing how many stones you might need to add to your water bottle to make your fish neutrally buoyant, or so that the bottle doesn't sink completely to the bottom or float to the surface.

3. Test your hypothesis by adding stones to the bottle and placing the bottle into the water-filled container. Did it sink to the bottom? Float to the top? Describe your results in your journal.

TIP:

➤ Leave the bottle for a few minutes to determine its position in the bucket. This allows for any external air bubbles to settle that may interfere with your results.

4. Adjust the number of stones in the bottle to achieve neutral buoyancy. Add more stones if your bottle floats, and take out stones if it sinks to the bottom. How many stones did you need to keep the bottle neutrally buoyant?

CONCLUSION:

In this activity you experimented to create neutral buoyancy in a plastic air-filled bottle. Fish create neutral buoyancy by maintaining the amount of gas within their swim bladders. By changing the rocks in your bottle, you adjusted the mass to create a model fish bladder that neither sinks nor floats. Fish achieve the same results by controlling the amount of gas in their swim bladders.

OCEAN JOURNAL ENTRY

This lesson taught you how a fish uses a swim bladder to maintain its position in the water column. Using what you have learned, answer the following questions in your journal.

1. *How many times did you need to adjust the number of stones in your bottle to achieve neutral buoyancy?*

2. *How long do you think it takes a fish to empty or fill their swim bladder?*

3. *If a fish lives on the bottom of the ocean, do you think it needs to have a swim bladder? Why or why not?*

FISH AND MARINE MAMMALS

LESSON

ANATOMY OF A JELLYFISH

Jellyfish are not actually a type of fish. They are part of a group of organisms called *cnidarians*, invertebrates with tentacles that have stinging cells. They are more closely related to corals and anemone, and are also considered a type of zooplankton because they are generally not strong swimmers and mostly drift on ocean currents. There are about 1,500 species of jellyfish, and they can be found in every ocean and at all depths.

The Anatomy of a JELLYFISH

- canals
- bell
- mouth
- muscles
- gonads
- eyespot
- gut
- tentacles
- oral arms with stinging cells

24 OCEAN ANATOMY ACTIVITIES FOR KIDS

LESSON

Jellies come in all shapes and sizes. The Australian box jellyfish, found in the warm waters of the Pacific, has one of the most deadly venoms on Earth and is considered the most venomous of all marine creatures. The lion's mane jellyfish is the largest-known species of jellyfish, with one specimen recorded at 8 feet (2.8 m) in diameter with tentacles up to 120 feet (36.5 m) long.

Jellyfish are remarkable animals with no heart, blood, or brains, and their bodies are made of approximately 95 percent water. Still, they can pump their *bell*, the bowl-shaped organ at the top of their bodies, to stay near the surface of the ocean. Most jellyfish even have eyespots located on their bell that can tell the difference between light and dark.

Jellyfish stomachs are located under their bell and they use tentacles to catch their food. Those tentacles contain millions of stinging cells, called *nematocysts*, that contain venom. The venom is released like a harpoon when the tentacles contact their prey. The venom paralyzes the prey. Jellyfish eat pretty much anything that gets caught in their tentacles, including some types of plankton, fish, or shrimp.

When jellyfish reproduce, they go through *metamorphosis*, like a butterfly. Baby jellyfish start as *polyps*, a stage of development in which the animal attaches upside down to the seafloor with tentacles extended upward. In later stages of its life cycle, a polyp releases a small juvenile jellyfish that will eventually grow into an adult.

Stinging Cells

Fun Fact

A group of jellyfish can be called a *swarm*, a *bloom*, or a *smack* if found in large groups.

FISH AND MARINE MAMMALS

ACTIVITY

MAKING A STINGING CELL

TIME:
10 TO 20 MINUTES

CATEGORY:
INDOOR, SIMULATION

MATERIALS
1 (8-OUNCE) PLASTIC CUP
BALLOON, NOT BLOWN UP
5 FEET YARN OR STRING
1 (1-INCH) POMPOM
TAPE

How do jellyfish release their venom? In this activity you will create your own version of a jellyfish stinging cell, and practice launching it in a similar way that jellyfish do.

Safety First! When launching your stinging cells be sure to work in an open area, avoiding other people.

PREP WORK

1. Cut off the bottom of the plastic cup.

2. Cut the balloon in half crosswise. Save the bottom piece with the balloon's neck attached.

STEP-BY-STEP INSTRUCTIONS

1. Slide the cut edge of the balloon over the bottomless half of the cup. Tie the neck of the balloon in a knot after it has been placed on the cup. This is going to be the outside of your stinging cell.

TIP:

➡ Be sure to hold the cup steady while releasing the tied end of the balloon.

26   OCEAN ANATOMY ACTIVITIES FOR KIDS

2. Tie one end of the string to the pompom. The pompom represents the venom inside the nematocyst.

3. Tape the other end of the string to the balloon from inside the cup. This will help illustrate the mechanism a nematocyst uses to inject venom in the jellyfish's prey.

4. Carefully wrap the string around the pompom and tuck it inside the cup.

5. Now comes the launch! Gently pull down on the tied end of the balloon while holding the cup. Imagine that a fish has just brushed up against a jellyfish tentacle. This is the signal to let go of the balloon and release the venom inside. What happens to the string and pompom? Record your observations in your journal.

CONCLUSION:

Jellyfish have some unique ways for obtaining food. Their stinging cells, nematocysts, inject venom into their prey, paralyzing it, so the jellyfish can have its meal. The model nematocyst that you created launched a pompom similar to the way that jellyfish use their nematocysts.

OCEAN JOURNAL ENTRY

You have just created your own version of a jellyfish stinging cell. Reflect on the activity as you answer the questions below.

1. *Since jellyfish don't have organs like sharp teeth or claws for catching prey, what is the advantage of having nematocysts?*

2. *Why do you think jellyfish have so many nematocysts in their tentacles?*

3. *Do you think a jellyfish can reload their nematocysts? If so, describe how you think they might do it.*

FISH AND MARINE MAMMALS

LESSON

ANATOMY OF A SHARK

There are more than 500 different species of shark. The largest species, the whale shark, can reach up to 39 feet (11.9 m) in length. At the other end of the spectrum, the smallest shark is the dwarf lantern shark, and it measures in at about 7.9 inches (20 cm), just over the size of an average adult hand.

Sharks are a type of fish called *elasmobranchs*. Elasmobranchs are unique among fish because their skeleton is made of cartilage instead of bone. Our ears are an example of an organ made of cartilage. Cartilage provides a lightweight, flexible support structure for sharks and other elasmobranchs, including stingrays and manta rays. In addition, it allows for quick movements to help them hunt, and the lighter skeleton helps them maintain buoyancy, since they don't have swim bladders like other fish.

Sharks can have anywhere from five to seven gill slits on each side of their head that help them breathe and even eat. Some sharks are predators and some are filter feeders. Instead of biting and chewing prey, filter feeders collect small particles of food from the water. Usually they do this by using specialized structures on their gills.

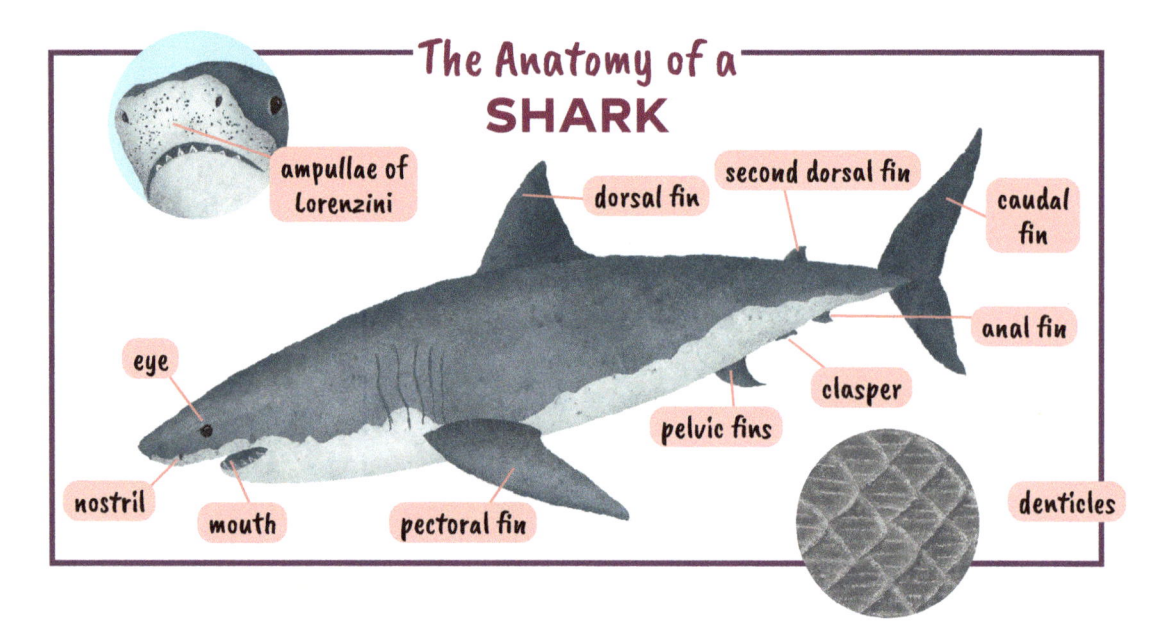

The Anatomy of a SHARK

- ampullae of Lorenzini
- dorsal fin
- second dorsal fin
- caudal fin
- anal fin
- clasper
- pelvic fins
- pectoral fin
- mouth
- nostril
- eye
- denticles

28　OCEAN ANATOMY ACTIVITIES FOR KIDS

LESSON

Unlike bony fish, sharks do not have gill covers. Water must continuously flow over their gills to extract oxygen so that they can breathe. A lot of sharks, like the great white and whale sharks, must keep swimming to keep water flowing over their gills to breathe, so they never stop moving. Other species, like the nurse shark, can pump water over their gills using their cheek muscles, or *buccal* muscles, and can be found resting at the seafloor sometimes.

Sharks that spend most of their time on the ocean floor are often called *carpet sharks*. These tend to have more flattened bodies with coloring that helps them camouflage. The tasselled wobbegong shark, found in the coral reefs of Australia and throughout the islands of Indonesia, has spotted coloring that blends in with the surrounding color. It even has special skin flaps that can cover its mouth and head, so the tasselled wobbegong can hide and attack when unsuspecting prey swim close by.

Some sharks, like the great white and mako shark, are built to be fierce ocean predators. These sharks' mouths contain rows of teeth that continuously replace themselves. If they lose one, there is another right behind it to take its place. They also usually have about eight fins, including large *dorsal fins* on top of their bodies, providing control and balance and making them fast in catching their prey. *Pectoral fins* on the sides of their body help them to make quick turns, and *caudal fins*, or tails, propel the shark through the water.

Aside from expertly crafted fins, sharks have other special features, like slim, torpedo-shaped bodies and *denticles* that help them increase their swimming speed. Denticles are super-tiny teeth-like scales with ridges and grooves that reduce the friction of water as it flows over the shark's skin. Together, the torpedo body shape and the denticles help the shark swim faster. Sharks with these body types tend to live in open ocean waters.

Fun Fact

Sharks have organs under their mouths called *ampullae of Lorenzini*. These organs can detect electrical currents given off by prey or items that might be hidden under sand or rocks.

FISH AND MARINE MAMMALS

ACTIVITY

SHARK SKIN

TIME:
15 TO 30 MINUTES

CATEGORY:
INDOOR, CRAFT

MATERIALS
DRAWING UTENSILS SUCH AS COLORED PENCILS, CRAYONS, OR MARKERS

2 TO 3 WHITE HARD-BOILED EGGS IN THEIR SHELL

PAPER

CLEAR-DRYING GLUE

In this activity you will use your imagination to design a shark to include dorsal, pectoral, and caudal fins. Using eggshells, you will add texture to your projects to represent denticles.

Safety First! *Be sure your hard-boiled eggs are completely cool before peeling them to avoid any burn injury.*

PREP WORK

1. Use markers to give the eggs some color. Choose colors you would like to have on a shark of your own design.

2. Peel the shell from the egg and crush it into small pieces.

STEP-BY-STEP INSTRUCTIONS

1. Consider the adaptations that sharks have that make them either excellent predators or filter feeders. Reflect on characteristics such as body shape as well as the number of fins, their size, and their shape. What will the shark's mouth look like?

2. On a sheet of paper, draw an outline of a shark, including details like the body shape, fin size and position, as well as the mouth. Color in your shark outline.

3. Once your drawing is complete, spread a thin layer of glue over your shark design, covering it completely.

4. Sprinkle the crushed eggshells over your shark. These will represent shark denticles.

TIP:
→ Instead of drawing on your eggs, you may dye or paint them to add your own artistic flair.

5. While the glue dries, describe your shark's scales, fins, skeleton, and body shape in your journal. How do these adaptations help them in the ocean?

whale shark

great white shark

nurse shark

bonnethead shark

CONCLUSION:
You drew a shark that has a lightweight skeleton of cartilage and a streamlined body shape. The eggshells you added to your shark design represent denticles, very small plate-like scales on the shark's skin that reduce the friction of water flow over its body as it swims.

OCEAN JOURNAL ENTRY

After creating your picture of a shark, reflect on the activity as you answer the questions below.

1. *Describe where your shark lives. Does it sit on the seafloor or swim in the open ocean? How is its body adapted for its environment?*

2. *Describe how your shark eats. Is it a filter feeder like the whale shark, or is it a predator like a great white?*

FISH AND MARINE MAMMALS

LESSON

ANATOMY OF A WHALE

Did you know whales are the largest animals on the planet? A blue whale can weigh as much as 400,000 pounds (181,437 kg) and can reach nearly 100 feet (30.5 m) long! Whales belong to a group of marine mammals called *cetaceans*. They have lungs and breathe air through blowholes on the tops of their bodies. Like other mammals, including humans, they give live birth and nurse their young. Many species inhabit arctic waters.

There are two kinds of whales: *toothed* and *baleen*. *Toothed whales* include dolphins, porpoises, and orcas. These whales have sharp teeth in their mouths for capturing their food. *Baleen whales*, like the blue whale and the

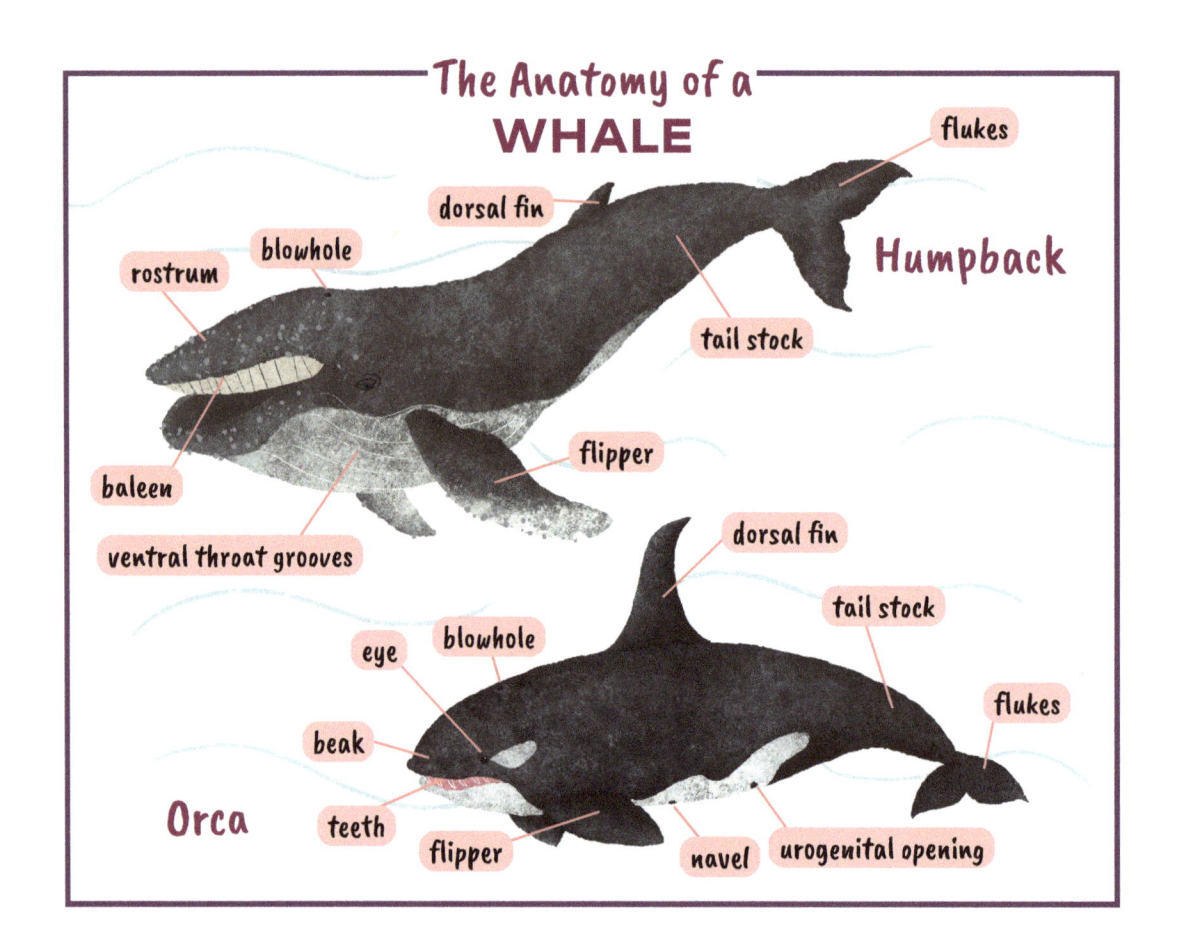

The Anatomy of a WHALE

Humpback
- flukes
- dorsal fin
- blowhole
- rostrum
- tail stock
- flipper
- baleen
- ventral throat grooves

Orca
- dorsal fin
- tail stock
- flukes
- blowhole
- eye
- beak
- teeth
- flipper
- navel
- urogenital opening

humpback, have structures in their mouth called baleen. Each piece of baleen resembles the bristly end of a broom. Baleen whales use these structures to filter their food from large gulps of water.

All mammals have some form of hair. Whales have much less hair than other mammals or they only have hair during one stage of their life. Dolphins, for example, have whiskers when they are born that disappear as they age, usually within a week. So, instead of large amounts of hair to keep warm in the ocean, whales have a thick layer of *blubber*. Blubber is a type of fat that keeps whale bodies warm in near freezing temperatures.

Since much of the ocean is dark, toothed whales have a unique sense called *echolocation* to find food. Echolocation is a process that allows whales to navigate and find prey using sound. Dolphins and orcas push air through their blowholes to create clicks and whistles. An organ in the whale's head called a *melon* directs the outgoing sound. Traveling quickly through water, these sounds bounce off of prey and return to the whale, similar to your voice echoing off a cave wall. The sounds are received in the fat-filled cavities of the whale's lower jaw. This information gives the whale the location of prey in the water.

Fun Fact

Some whales can sing! Baleen whales, like the humpback, can create a wide range of clicks and whistles called *whale song*. These sounds aren't used for echolocation, though. Rather, researchers believe that humpbacks use their songs to communicate with one another.

ACTIVITY

WHALE SENSES GAME

TIME:
10 TO 20 MINUTES

CATEGORY:
OUTDOOR, GAME

MATERIALS
LARGE OPEN OUTDOOR AREA

2 TO 4 PLAYERS

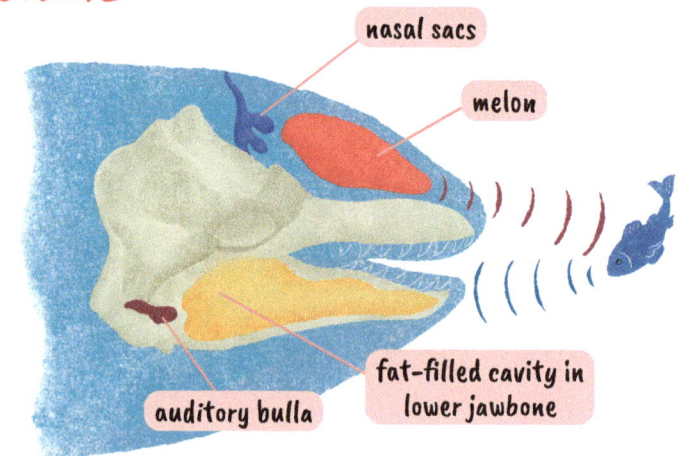

BLINDFOLD

Diagram labels: nasal sacs, melon, fat-filled cavity in lower jawbone, auditory bulla

In this activity you will stretch your senses to experience what it is like for a whale to find their food using echolocation. You will need to rely on your sense of hearing to find your fellow players while blindfolded. The object of the game is for the whale player to use their sense of hearing to "tag" the fish players.

Safety First! Choose an open play area that is safe from any dangerous objects or moving vehicles, such as your backyard or a playground.

PREP WORK

1. Clear the play area of unsafe obstacles that a blindfolded player may trip over.

2. Decide which player will be first as the blindfolded whale and which players will be fish.

TIP:

→ You can change the level of difficulty of the game by allowing fish players to move during the game and allowing the whale players unlimited calls.

34 OCEAN ANATOMY ACTIVITIES FOR KIDS

STEP-BY-STEP INSTRUCTIONS

1. Begin by moving the whale player to the middle of the play area and blindfolding them.

2. Once the whale player is unable to see, the fish players will scatter out over the playing area representing fish within the ocean. Fish players may not move after they have picked a spot.

3. The whale player locates fish players by listening for their responses to his or her calls. When the whale player yells, "Echo!" all fish players must respond, "Location!"

4. Whale players may only call a total of 10 times in a game. If a fish player is caught, the game ends and the caught fish becomes the whale for the next round.

CONCLUSION:

You have just experienced how some whales use echolocation in the ocean. Relying on your sense of hearing to identify the location of fish players using a calling system is similar to the way the whale uses an echo to find food in the dark ocean.

OCEAN JOURNAL ENTRY

In this activity, you learned what it is like to find objects using echolocation. Reflect on your experience playing the game as you answer the questions below.

1. *What advantage does echolocation give whales when finding their prey?*

2. *Describe how our sense of hearing is similar to the echolocation of a whale. How is it different?*

FISH AND MARINE MAMMALS

The Anatomy of a KELP FOREST

- mackerel
- sea otter
- garibaldi fish
- sea lion
- sea urchin
- abalone
- sunflower sea star
- red algae

COASTS AND SHORELINES

3

This chapter brings us to the place where ocean meets land: coastlines and shorelines. A *coastline* is the area of land from high tide toward land, and a *shoreline* is the area of ocean waters from high tide toward the ocean. Rocky cliffs and sandy beaches create diverse and dynamic habitats. Coastlines and shorelines constantly change with tide and wave action. Since sea level changes with the tides, the place between high and low tide is called the *intertidal zone*. This chapter explores the ways shorelines are created and changed while looking at some of the diverse habitats that can be found there.

LESSON

ANATOMY OF A BEACH

A day at the beach often means feeling sand between your toes and listening to the sound of waves crashing on the shore. What creates these beautiful places we love to travel to? This lesson explores how beaches form, what they are made of, and the types of organisms that can be found there.

Beaches, the narrow strips of land found at the transition between the coastline and shoreline, are usually made of sand, or rocks broken down into incredibly small pieces. The rocks break down and form sand during a process called *weathering*, when waves crash onto a beach or rocks, wearing them down. *Erosion* occurs when these particles are moved from their place of origin. Waves erode beaches when they move sand along the shoreline though *longshore currents,* or currents that move parallel to the shoreline, which are formed as waves crash and then pull back out to sea along the shoreline.

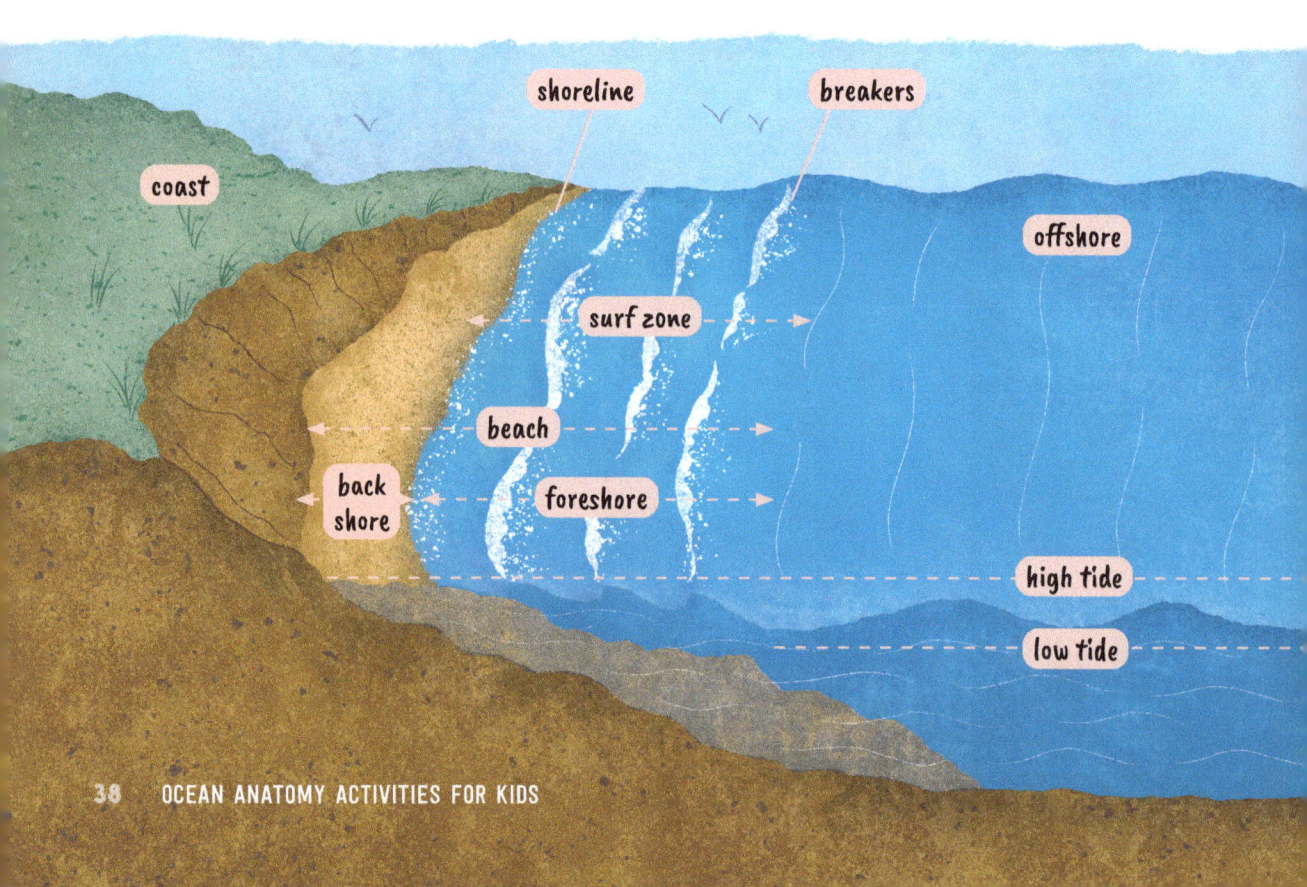

LESSON

While there are many different types of sandy beaches, sand is not the only thing that can make up a beach. Beaches can be made of pebbles, rocks, boulders, and even seashells! The color of sand at a beach is determined by the type of *sediment* it is made from. Sediments are small particles of solid material moved by wind and water. For example, you can find many black sand beaches on the Hawaiian Islands because of the often-black lava that makes up the islands themselves. The whitest beach in the world, according to Guinness World Records, is Hyams Beach in Australia. The sand at this beach is made primarily of quartz.

Beaches provide a habitat for several different species of birds worldwide. Many will nest along the coastline and feed on the rich sea life on the shore. Some of the more common birds found on beaches include seagulls, pelicans, and sandpipers. Pelicans, using their large bill, gulp down surface seawater containing fish. The American white pelican's throat pouch can hold up to 3 gallons of water!

Ghost crabs, also known as sand crabs, are a common resident of many tropical and subtropical sandy beaches. They live in intricate burrows and usually tunnel through the sandy intertidal zone.

Fun Fact

Adult parrotfish can create up to 1,000 pounds (450 kg) of sand per year by chewing on coral with their beak-like jaw. Once in their gut, the coral is ground up even further and eliminated as sand!

ACTIVITY

CHANGING BEACHES

TIME:
10 TO 20 MINUTES

CATEGORY:
INDOOR, EXPERIMENT

MATERIALS
SHALLOW 9-BY-13-INCH METAL PAN

SAND, GRAVEL, AND STONES (TO ACT AS YOUR SEDIMENT)

12-OUNCE WATER BOTTLE FILLED WITH WATER AND CLOSED

SPRAY BOTTLE FILLED WITH WATER

WATER

How does rain and wave action affect beach formation? In this activity you will experiment with different forms of water erosion to observe their effects on beach sediment.

PREP WORK

1. Gather materials to work in an area you don't mind getting wet.

2. Create a beach on one side of the pan by placing the sand in a pile reaching to the top of the pan. Your beach model should slope down toward the middle of the pan.

3. Once your beach has been created, fill the pan with water until it reaches halfway up the side of the pan.

STEP-BY-STEP INSTRUCTIONS

1. First, we will examine how rain affects the erosion of a beach. Begin by spraying the top of your beach with the spray bottle until you notice water gathering and running down the slope of your beach. Where does the water travel? How did it change the shape of your beach? Record your observations in your journal.

2. Next, we will explore how wave action affects the erosion of a beach. Lay the sealed water bottle on the water side of the pan parallel to the beach. Slowly roll the water bottle toward the beach along the bottom of the pan. This will simulate waves hitting the shoreline. What happens to the beach? Record your observations in your journal.

40   OCEAN ANATOMY ACTIVITIES FOR KIDS

3. Roll the water bottle faster. What happened to the beach? How is this different than the first time you created waves with the water bottle? Record your observations in your journal.

4. Once you have completed each step, repeat the experiment again but change the position and type of materials used for the beach. What changed after conducting the experiment the second time? What stayed the same?

TIP:
➤ Allow the water to settle in your experiment before increasing your waves' speed.

OCEAN JOURNAL ENTRY

Reflect on the simulation of rain and waves on your beach model as you answer the questions below.

1. *Did you observe a relationship between the amount of rain an area receives and the amount of erosion? Explain why.*

2. *Did you observe a relationship between the strength of the waves hitting the beach and the amount of erosion? Explain why.*

3. *In what ways did changing the composition of your beach change your experiment's results?*

CONCLUSION:
This activity simulated some of the physical forces that create and keep shaping beaches. Beaches are created from the weathering and erosion of rocks and other materials, such as shells. Wind, rain, and waves are some of the forces behind this process. The spray bottle of water simulated rain's effects on beach erosion. By rolling the water bottle through the model you were able to observe how wave action affects erosion. Together, these forces make the beach a *dynamic* landform, meaning it's constantly changing.

COASTS AND SHORELINES

LESSON

TIDE POOLS

One unique place to observe marine life is in a *tide pool*. They contain organisms within a specific space, like a natural aquarium. On the Pacific Coast of the United States, tide pools can be quite colorful, harboring purple sea urchins, orange sea stars, and the giant green anemone. The giant green anemone is related to jellyfish and gets some of its green color from the relationship it has with the microalgae and *dinoflagellates*, also considered a type of algae, living inside of it.

LESSON

Tide pools are created by rocky depressions on shorelines in the intertidal zone, like miniature valleys. When the tide moves out to sea, this "valley" remains filled with water, making it an isolated pool. The seawater in tide pools is regularly refreshed when the tide rises. *Seaweed*, the common name of many species of large marine algae, covers rocks in green, red, and brown mats. These mats float like tangles of hair when the tide is in and seawater covers these pools.

Creatures that live in a tide pool are subject to dramatic physical changes throughout a tidal cycle. At low tide, tide pool organisms have an increased risk of becoming dinner for someone else, and some may even be exposed to the air! Crabs and wading birds search these exposed pools for food. Humans can also disrupt these small ecosystems, so it's important when visiting to not touch.

Also when the tide is low, organisms are cut off from a fresh seawater supply and temperatures in the pool can rise quickly from sun exposure. Oxygen levels can drop dramatically, and animals risk drying out. But animals that are permanently attached to the shoreline have adaptations to withstand their time on dry land. Barnacles, a type of crustacean related to crabs, stay permanently attached to their position in the tide pool. They can close up their shell tightly to keep from drying out when exposed to the air.

When the tide rises again to cover the tide pool and replenish the seawater, waves pound the rocks with incredible force, threatening to pull animals away from their habitat. To keep from being washed out to sea by wave action, tide pool organisms have the ability to produce a tight grip on intertidal rocks. Animals like sea stars and urchins hold onto rocks using thousands of tiny feet-like suction cups.

Fun Fact

Barnacles produce a cement-like material to help them stay put in a tide pool. Scientists consider it to be one of the most powerful natural glues in existence!

ACTIVITY

CREATE A TIDE POOL

WAIT TIME:
1 TO 2 DAYS

CATEGORY:
INDOOR, CRAFT

MATERIALS
NEWSPAPER TO COVER A WORKSTATION

DISPOSABLE PAPER BOWL

ALUMINUM FOIL

ROLLING PIN

1 TO 2 POUNDS OF AIR-DRY CLAY

RULER

WASHABLE ACRYLIC PAINT (SEVERAL COLORS)

PAINT BRUSHES

SCHOOL GLUE (LIKE ELMER'S)

In this activity, you will create a sculpture of a tide pool from clay. Using what you have learned about the tide pool habitat, add details to the tide pool, including the animals and seaweed that inhabit these waters.

PREP WORK

1. Cover your workstation with newspaper to keep it clean.

2. Place the paper bowl upside down on the newspaper and cover it with aluminum foil.

STEP-BY-STEP INSTRUCTIONS

1. Begin by rolling out your clay into a circle about ½ inch thick and approximately 2 inches wider than the diameter of the top of the bowl. You can measure this by laying your bowl upside down on top of the rolled-out clay. Cut the clay to the right size.

2. Once you have your clay piece cut, lay the clay circle on top of the aluminum foil on the upside-down bowl. Press the clay down to mold it to the shape of the bowl.

3. Using leftover clay, create three-dimensional sculptures of some of the creatures that live in tide pools, such as barnacles, anemone, and sea stars.

4. Allow the air-dry clay bowl and the animal sculptures to harden overnight.

5. Once all the clay sculptures are fully dry, carefully flip over the bowl and remove both the bowl and the aluminum foil from the inside of the clay. This is the base of your tide pool.

6. It's time to bring your tide pool to life! Paint rocks and seaweed inside of your tide pool base. Paint the animal sculptures to give them color too. Allow these to dry for 1 to 2 hours.

7. Use glue to attach the animals to the inside of the tide pool base. Once the glue is dry, just like the tube feet of sea stars and the glue of barnacles, it will keep the animals in place.

OCEAN JOURNAL ENTRY

In this activity, you created a sculpture of a tide pool and added organisms to reflect the ecosystem that can be found there. Use your experience from the creation of your sculpture to help you answer the questions below.

1. *Describe some of the ways the environment of a tide pool changes drastically throughout the day.*

2. *Describe the adaptations that animals like barnacles and sea stars must have to help them stay put in the tide pool ecosystem.*

3. *How is your model of a tide pool similar to or different from the tide pools you might find along the coast?*

CONCLUSION:

In this activity, you created a sculpture of a tide pool. The clay bowl represents the depressions found along rocky coastlines that create the tide pool ecosystem. Gluing your animals to your sculpture represents the way that the animals found in tide pools can tightly stick to the tide pool's rock surfaces to avoid being swept out to sea with the tide.

TIPS:

➡ Applying an acrylic sealer will help preserve your sculpture after it has been painted.

➡ Store air-dry clay in a sealed container with a small amount of water to keep it from drying out.

COASTS AND SHORELINES

LESSON

ANATOMY OF A KELP FOREST

Imagine an underwater forest teeming with life. That's a *kelp forest*! Kelp forests can be found in cool waters around the world, but especially along the Pacific Coast of North America. The collection of kelp towers that make up these forests provides food and shelter for thousands of marine species. In this lesson, you will journey into a kelp forest to discover both what creates them and what animals call the kelp forest home.

Giant kelp is a species of large brown algae. There are more than 30 species of kelp that can be found in kelp forests, but giant kelp is the largest species of kelp—and algae—on the planet. It often reaches heights of 100 feet (30 m), and forms the towering structures that are characteristic of Pacific Coast kelp forests. In ideal conditions, giant kelp can grow up to 2 feet (0.6 m) in just one day! Like other algae, kelp can photosynthesize to create energy, so it needs to remain in the sunlight zone of the ocean.

Like forests on land, a kelp forest has a *canopy*, an *understory*, and a *forest floor*, but kelp forests face some unique challenges. The wave action that exists along the rocky shoreline can often threaten to wash the kelp out to sea. Giant kelp has four basic structures to help it survive in turbulent waters. *Holdfasts* at the bottom of the kelp attach to rocky earth, creating a cement-like

46   OCEAN ANATOMY ACTIVITIES FOR KIDS

hold. Stem-like structures called *stipes* help the kelp grow upward, and blades on the stipes, similar to leaves, help giant kelp absorb sunlight to keep growing. Finally, giant kelp uses floats, called *air bladders*, to keep itself upright.

Adorable sea otters can be found at the surface floating through the kelp canopy, anchoring themselves to the kelp while they sleep. They feast on invertebrates such as sea urchins, which in turn munch on the kelp itself. Large sea otters can eat up to 25 pounds (11.3 kg) of food a day! The sea otter's consumption of urchins keeps the sea urchin population balanced. Urchins can help clean up fallen kelp, but if they are left on their own, they can destroy a kelp forest.

Otters are not the only marine mammals found in these forests. Sea lions and seals feed on the fish here, and gray whales can be found filter feeding while they keep safe from predators like killer whales.

Fun Fact

There are more than 100 different species of rock fish near kelp forest habitats. They are one of the longest-living fish species.

ACTIVITY

KEEPING KELP AFLOAT

TIME:
20 TO 30 MINUTES

CATEGORY:
INDOOR, MODEL

MATERIALS
CRAYONS (GREEN AND BROWN)
12-BY-12-INCH SQUARE OF WAX PAPER
RULER
SCISSORS
1 TO 3 MINI MARSHMALLOWS
STAPLER
ONE ROCK, ABOUT THE DIAMETER OF A QUARTER
CLOTHESPIN
EMPTY 2-LITER BOTTLE WITH THE TOP CUT OFF
WATER

In this activity, you will create a model that teaches you about the giant kelp's four basic structures—holdfast, stipe, blades, and air bladder.

PREP WORK

1. Gather materials to work in an area you don't mind getting wet.

2. Using crayons, draw and color a giant kelp on a piece of wax paper that is approximately 8 inches tall and no more than 3 inches wide. Make sure it includes a holdfast, stipe, and blades.

3. Label the structures on your diagram based on the illustration on page 46.

4. Cut out your kelp diagram from the wax paper.

5. Wrap the top of your kelp diagram around the mini marshmallow and staple it closed. Since marshmallows are filled with air, the marshmallow will act as an air bladder for your kelp model.

6. Wrap the holdfast at the bottom of the diagram around the rock and use the clothespin to secure it in place. The clothespin holds on to the rock and the wax paper diagram just like kelp holdfast holds on to the rocky seafloor. You now have a complete kelp model!

STEP-BY-STEP INSTRUCTIONS

1. Place your kelp model inside of the 2-liter bottle. Notice how it folds toward the bottom without water. Predict what will happen when it is submerged under water.

2. Slowly pour water into the container until the kelp is completely submerged. What happened to the kelp? Record your observations in your journal.

> **TIP:**
> ➤ You may wrap more than one blade around the mini marshmallow if you are having trouble getting it to stay attached to the diagram.

OCEAN JOURNAL ENTRY

In this activity you created a model of a giant kelp including its four basic structures—holdfast, stipe, blade, and air bladder. These structures are important for the kelp to create the habitat for so many organisms. Use your model as a reference to help you answer the following questions in your journal.

1. *What happened to the kelp once it was submerged underwater? Describe why you think this happened.*

2. *Describe the importance of the holdfast and the air bladder structures of kelp.*

3. *Describe how a kelp forest is similar to a forest that can be found on land.*

CONCLUSION:
In this lesson, you created a model of a giant kelp. Building these structures showed you how giant kelp are designed to grow in large, upright towers that withstand wave action and provide an essential habitat to so many species.

COASTS AND SHORELINES

The Anatomy of a CORAL REEF

- sea turtle
- sea fan coral
- stingray
- angelfish
- button polyps
- soft coral
- parrotfish
- staghorn coral
- sea slug
- anemone

CORAL REEFS

A coral reef is a submerged habitat that provides shelter for other organisms to eat and grow. The "tropical rainforests of the sea," they are the most diverse of all shallow-water marine ecosystems. They are estimated to contain nearly a quarter of all known species in the ocean! There are four different types: barrier reefs, patch reefs, fringing reefs, and atolls. *Barrier reefs* can be found offshore, near coastlines. They are separated from the shoreline by bodies of water called *lagoons* and often reach the ocean's surface. *Patch reefs* grow in shallow areas within lagoons. *Fringing reefs* begin closer to the shoreline and grow out toward the sea. Fringing reefs that keep growing around islands that are submerged in the ocean form a circular reef called an *atoll*.

LESSON

ANATOMY OF A CORAL REEF

coral body

polyps

Coral reefs are created by tiny animals, related to jellyfish, called *coral polyps*. These polyps can live individually or in larger colonies that can take up a lot of space. Polyps have delicate bodies. They grow their skeleton on the outside of their bodies using calcium and carbonate ions from seawater. There are two types of corals: *soft coral* and *hard coral*. Soft corals form flexible skeletons that look more like plants. While they live in coral reefs, they are not considered reef builders. However, hard corals, also known as *stony corals*, continuously grow hard skeletons, gradually building up and outward. There are more than 3,000 species of stony corals, and they each form a different size and shape. When stony corals die, their hard skeletons remain intact. New corals can grow on top of these stony coral skeletons, gradually building up the reef. It may take hundreds or even thousands of years, but eventually this process makes the large coral reefs we see in oceans today.

LESSON

Coral polyps usually have a clear body, but they can be quite colorful due to a photosynthetic algae living inside of them. These algae, called *zooxanthellae*, have a symbiotic relationship with the coral. A *mutualistic* or *symbiotic relationship* is one in which two different organisms benefit from each other. In the example of coral and zooxanthellae, the coral provides a home for the algae and the algae create essential energy for the coral. Some soft corals have the zooxanthellae, but stony corals require them to survive. Sometimes corals expel their zooxanthellae due to stress caused by a rise in ocean temperature. This is life-threatening for the coral: They lose their color, become white, and can eventually die if they don't recover. This is known as *coral bleaching*. Conservationists are working on combatting coral bleaching events from increased sea temperatures and other reef threats, including overfishing and water pollution, in order to protect these ecosystems. Many animals that live on a reef have evolved to mimic their colorful surroundings. For example, many pygmy seahorse species live exclusively on corals and hold a striking resemblance to their hosts—corals. These tiny seahorses grow no larger than an inch in length, and some are as small as a grain of rice. Because they are incredibly small and so well camouflaged, new species of pygmy seahorses have only recently been discovered.

Fun Fact

The Great Barrier Reef, the largest coral reef in the world, is located off the Australian coast. It is so large that it can be seen from space.

ACTIVITY

CORAL REEF ROCK CANDY

WAIT TIME:
1 TO 5 DAYS

SET UP TIME:
30 MINUTES

CATEGORY:
SIMULATION

MATERIALS
2 (3-CM) PIECES OF CIRCULAR-SHAPED HARD CANDY

2 TO 3 TABLESPOONS OF GRANULATED SUGAR ON A PLATE

3-QUART SAUCEPAN

1 CUP OF WATER

3 CUPS OF GRANULATED SUGAR

2 (16-OUNCE) MASON JARS

FUNNEL

FOOD COLORING

In this activity, you will simulate coral reef growth with the creation of rock candy! New corals can grow on top of established coral skeletons similar to the way that sugar crystals grow on established crystals in the formation of rock candy.

Safety First! *Use extreme caution when boiling water to avoid burns. Have an adult help you.*

PREP WORK

Wet the hard candy with water. While wet, roll the candy on the plate of granulated sugar, covering it completely. Set the candy aside to dry while you create the solution. Imagine that this sugar coating will become the first layer of a coral colony to settle on a reef.

STEP-BY-STEP INSTRUCTIONS

1. In a saucepan over medium heat, heat the water.

2. Once the water begins to simmer, add 1 cup of sugar at a time, stirring it until each cup dissolves completely before adding the next.

3. Heat until the solution begins to boil, constantly stirring the whole time.

4. Once the solution has reached a boil, remove it from the heat and allow it to cool for 20 minutes. Drop in a few drops of food coloring and stir to combine.

5. Arrange one hard candy at the bottom of each mason jar, leaving at least 2 inches of space between the candy and the sides of the jar. Imagine these are coral colonies growing on a reef.

6. After the solution has cooled, use the funnel to pour the solution into each jar. Imagine that this solution is seawater filled with the nutrients for stony corals to grow.

7. Now it's time to let your coral reef grow! Coral reefs take hundreds of years to mature, but your rock candy reef should form in about five days. Check on your reef once a day to observe any changes that have occurred. Write your observations in your journal.

CONCLUSION:

This activity simulated the growth of a coral reef. Sugar crystals represented coral. Just as rock candy grew from the sugar crystals at the start of your reef, corals grow their structures on top of older coral skeletons. Over time stony corals build to form large reefs. Similarly, the sugar crystals in your rock candy reef grew to form larger pieces.

TIP:

➡ If you would like different colored corals, divide the sugar solution evenly, then add 2 to 4 drops of food coloring to each one. Separate the candies into different mason jars, adding the colored solution you choose for each one.

OCEAN JOURNAL ENTRY

New sugar crystals growing on the existing crystals on the hard candy mimics the way that stony corals grow to form large reefs. Use your experience from this activity to answer the questions below.

1. *Hard corals build their skeletons out of a chemical called calcium carbonate found in sea water. The crystals of rock candy grew from the sugar dissolved in solution. How is their growth similar or different from each other?*

2. *Describe the symbiotic relationship between zooxanthellae and coral polyps. Why is this relationship important to corals?*

CORAL REEFS

LESSON

SEA STARS

In this lesson, we will examine the anatomy of one of the coral reef's inhabitants, the sea star. Sea stars, also known as starfish, are not actually fish, just like jellyfish aren't fish. Sea stars are part of a group of invertebrates called *echinoderms*, animals that have an *endoskeleton*. The endoskeleton is a hard internal structure made of calcium carbonate plates. Echinoderms have a thin layer of "skin" called the *epidermis* that covers the endoskeleton. The term "echinoderm" means *spiny skin*, which refers to the bumpy texture of these soft-bodied creatures.

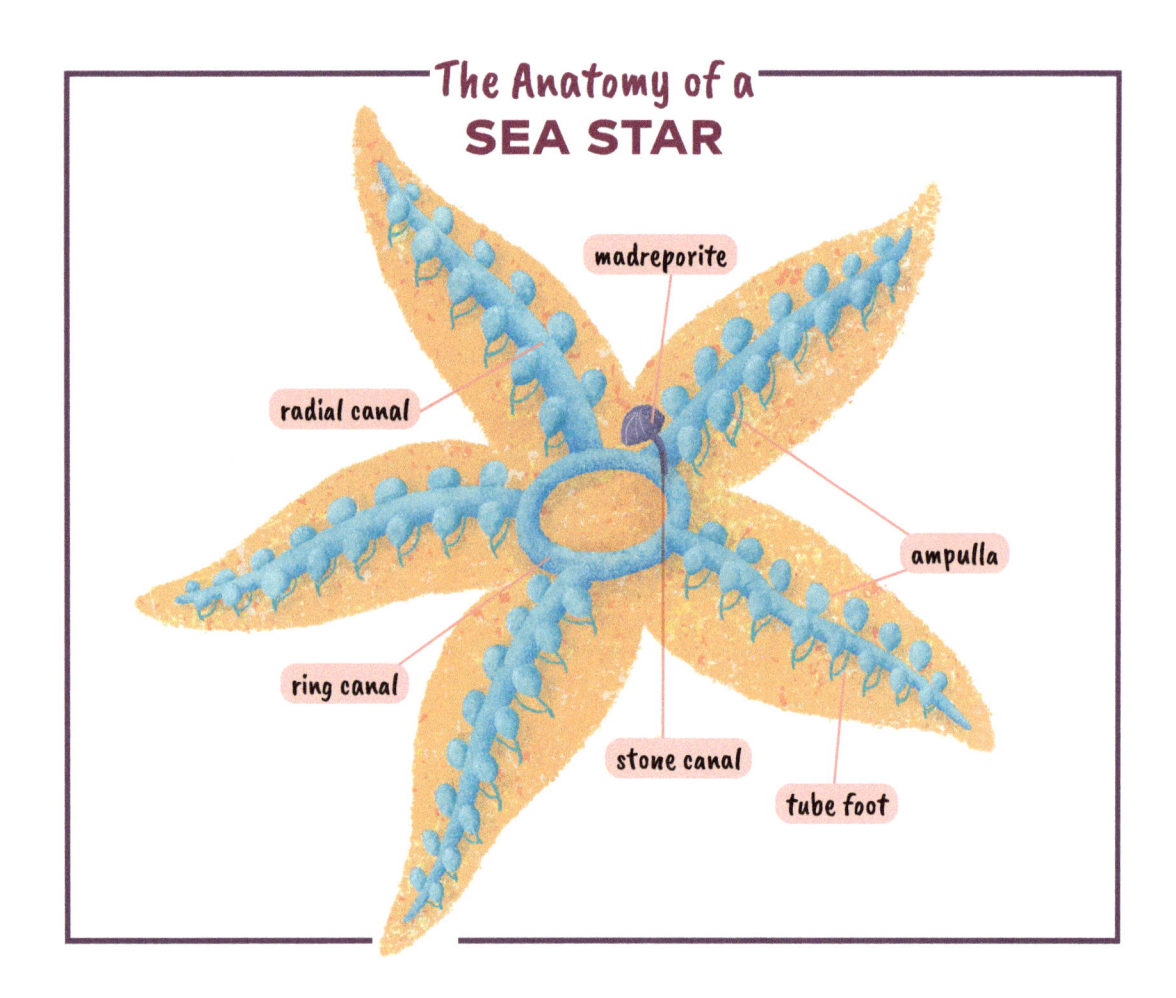

The Anatomy of a SEA STAR

- madreporite
- radial canal
- ampulla
- ring canal
- stone canal
- tube foot

56 OCEAN ANATOMY ACTIVITIES FOR KIDS

LESSON

Sea stars have no brain, heart, or blood. Instead, they have an internal water vascular, or circulatory, system made of a series of water-filled tubes that the animals use to transport materials throughout their bodies. Muscle contractions cause pressure that moves water through these tubes to the hundreds of delicate tube feet on the underside of their bodies. These feet then are able to attach to surfaces like a suction cup, move, and capture prey. Sea stars also breathe by taking in oxygen through their tube feet.

A sea star pushes its stomach out of its body to consume its food. Most sea stars are predatory, seeking mollusks, like clams and oysters, to eat. The crown-of-thorns starfish eats coral. This sea star can eat more than 42 square feet (13 m^2) of coral in one year. When the population of these sea stars gets out of control, they can cause serious damage to coral reefs. The most well-known predator of the crown-of-thorns starfish is the Pacific triton, a type of sea snail.

There are more than 2,000 species of sea stars, and most have five limbs—though not all. The cushion sea star's arms are reduced in size, which makes it appear round instead of star shaped. The largest sea star, the sunflower sea star, has anywhere from 15 to 24 limbs and can grow more than 3 feet (1 m) across. With this many limbs, it can move at a rate of more than 3 feet (1 m) per minute!

Fun Fact

Sea stars have the remarkable power to regrow portions of their body as adults. Some species can grow a whole new sea star from one lost limb.

CORAL REEFS 57

ACTIVITY

SEA STAR FEET

TIME:
15 TO 30 MINUTES

ACTIVITY CATEGORY:
INDOOR, EXPERIMENT

MATERIALS
1 (8-OUNCE) CLEAR GLASS
WATER
1 PENNY
1 COTTON BALL
1 DRY BEAN OR PEANUT
1 TURKEY BASTER
TIMER OR A WATCH WITH A SECOND HAND

TIP:

→ Try exploring how the turkey baster holds other submerged materials that you may have in your house. Record times for each new material in the data table in your journal. Do you notice any patterns?

Sea stars move using hundreds of tiny tube feet located on the underside of their bodies. These tube feet also enable the sea star to suction itself to surfaces. In this activity, you will use a turkey baster to model how a sea star's tube feet might grasp different surfaces. A single turkey baster represents one tube foot of the many hundred that each sea star has.

PREP WORK

1. Gather your materials to work in an area you don't mind getting wet.

2. Create a table in your journal with the following column headings: Penny, Bean, and Cotton Ball.

STEP-BY-STEP INSTRUCTIONS

1. Fill the glass two-thirds full of water.

2. Submerge the penny, cotton ball, and bean (or peanut) at the bottom of the glass of water.

3. Squeeze the rubber bulb of the turkey baster and hold it.

4. Submerge the end of the turkey baster into the glass of water.

5. Still squeezing the rubber bulb, place the tip of the turkey baster directly on top of the penny.

6. Release the rubber bulb and gently lift the turkey baster up from the bottom of the glass. What happened to the penny? Did it stick to the tip of the baster?

OCEAN ANATOMY ACTIVITIES FOR KIDS

7. Try this process again. Time how long the penny sticks to the tip of the baster after you release the bulb. In the table in your journal, record how long the baster held on to the penny.

8. Repeat steps 3 through 7, except this time, place the tip of the turkey baster on the bean. How was it the same as or different from the penny?

9. Lastly, repeat steps 3 through 7 again, but place the tip of the turkey baster on the cotton ball. How did this experience compare with the bean and penny?

OCEAN JOURNAL ENTRY

This activity allowed you to explore the way sea stars use their tube feet. Reflect on your experience as you answer the following questions in your journal.

1. *In your own words, describe how sea stars use pressure changes to grab onto surfaces.*

2. *Does the type of surface affect the time an object can be held by the turkey baster? What might this mean for a sea star's ability to grab on to surfaces?*

3. *What are some advantages of having tube feet like the sea star?*

CONCLUSION:

You have just explored how pressure changes within a closed tube, like that of a sea star's feet, grab on to different surfaces. When you squeezed the bulb of the turkey baster, this reduced pressure inside the tube. Higher pressure outside the tube pushes objects onto the tip of the baster, causing it to grip. Sea stars contract muscles inside their bodies to reduce internal pressure around their tube feet. Higher pressure outside the feet allows those feet to form a grip on surfaces. Each sea star's tube foot is small compared to the whole animal. However, with hundreds or even thousands of these feet spread out under the animal, it can create a grip strong enough to move itself through the water.

CORAL REEFS

LESSON

SEA TURTLES

Sea turtles are air-breathing reptiles that spend their whole lives in the ocean and are one of the many *vertebrates*, or animals with a backbone, that rely on the coral reef habitat for food. There are seven different species of sea turtle: leatherback, loggerhead, green, hawksbill, flatback, olive ridley, and Kemp's ridley.

Just like freshwater turtles, most sea turtles, except for the leatherback, have a hard shell called a *carapace*. However, instead of legs and claws like freshwater turtles, they have flippers. You may have seen a freshwater turtle pull its head and legs inside of its shell for protection, but sea turtles do not have the space inside their shell to retract their heads or limbs.

Hawksbill sea turtles, a medium-size species of sea turtle famous for their golden-brown shell and beak-like mouth, are frequent visitors to coral reefs. Here they seek shelter and search for food. They love to munch on sea sponges. Sea sponges are invertebrates that can often be found tucked into cracks and crevices of the reef. The hawksbill uses its pointy mouth to reach the sponges. The hawksbill can consume more than 1,000 pounds (453.6 kg) of sponges a year. It keeps the sponge population in check and prevents them from overrunning important reef-building corals.

LESSON

Sea turtles leave the ocean only to lay their eggs. Depending on the species, sea turtles lay eggs once every two to three years, or as often as once a year. During a nesting season, 65 to 180 eggs are laid two to six times, in two-week intervals. The eggs incubate in the nest for approximately two months.

Hatchlings usually leave the nest in a group during the night. The moon's reflection off the ocean guides sea turtle hatchlings toward the sea. Traveling across the beach into the shallow waters of the ocean in the cover of darkness helps them to avoid predators such as birds and large fish, but this tactic is not always successful. It's estimated that only 1 percent of hatchlings survive to adulthood.

Fun Fact

Female sea turtles return to the beach they were born on to lay their eggs. Researchers believe that they use the magnetic field of the Earth to find their way. This sense is called *magnetoreception*.

ACTIVITY

SURVIVAL OF SEA TURTLES

TIME:
10 TO 20 MINUTES

CATEGORY:
INDOOR, GAME

MATERIALS
2 (16-OUNCE) PAPER CUPS

CRAYONS OR MARKERS

20 MINI MARSHMALLOWS (OR JELLY BEANS)

1 (6-SIDED) DICE

Sea turtle hatchlings have many threats to their survival. They can become a meal for a hungry predator or get entangled in fishing gear. Sea turtles confuse plastic pollution for food and become sick after eating it. Human activity on beaches also disrupts their nesting grounds. In this activity, you will simulate the survival of sea turtle hatchlings after leaving the nest.

PREP WORK

1. Label one paper cup "1: Nesting Beach." Feel free to get creative and draw a sea turtle nest on the side of the cup.

2. Label the other cup "2: Threats." List or draw some of the threats to sea turtles, such as predators, entanglement, fishing, plastic ingestion, and beach erosion.

STEP-BY-STEP INSTRUCTIONS

1. Begin with all the mini marshmallows outside of the cups. Each marshmallow represents a hatchling about to leave the nest. Knowing each hatchling faces several threats, predict how many of the 20 will survive.

2. Select a hatchling and roll the dice to determine its fate. If you roll a **1**, the hatchling is placed in the nesting beach cup. These hatchlings survived to return to their home beach to nest. If you roll a number **2 through 6**, the hatchling is placed in the threats cup. These hatchlings do not survive.

TIP:

➡ Pretend that you have eliminated some threats to sea turtle survival by reducing plastic pollution. Repeat the experiment, this time changing the rules. Sea turtles for which you roll the numbers 1 and 2 will be placed in the survival cup.

3. Repeat this process for all 20 hatchlings. Compare the number of hatchlings in each cup. Write your observations in your journal.

4. Repeat the experiment after recording your results. How was this simulation the same as or different from the first?

OCEAN JOURNAL ENTRY:

This activity provided you with an opportunity to experience the probability of sea turtle survival. Use your experience from the activity to help you answer the questions below.

1. *How many of the hatchlings made it to their home beach? Is this greater than or less than the number that were captured by threats? How does it compare to your hypothesis?*

2. *Find the percentage of your sea turtles that survived by dividing the number that survived by 20 and multiplying your answer by 100. How does this percentage compare to the true survival rate of 1 percent?*

3. *Human activity that creates pollution and beach disruption is a threat to sea turtle survival. Write down some ways humans might be able help sea turtles.*

CONCLUSION:

Sea turtles hatch on sandy beaches, and then they return to their home beach to lay their eggs as adults. This activity explored the probability of hatchling survival. Due to many threats from human activity or natural predators, most do not survive to adulthood. In this simulation, using a 6-sided dice, the survival rate was less than 17 percent. In the wild, sea turtles are thought to have a much lower survival rate of 1 percent.

CORAL REEFS

The Anatomy of the OCEAN FLOOR

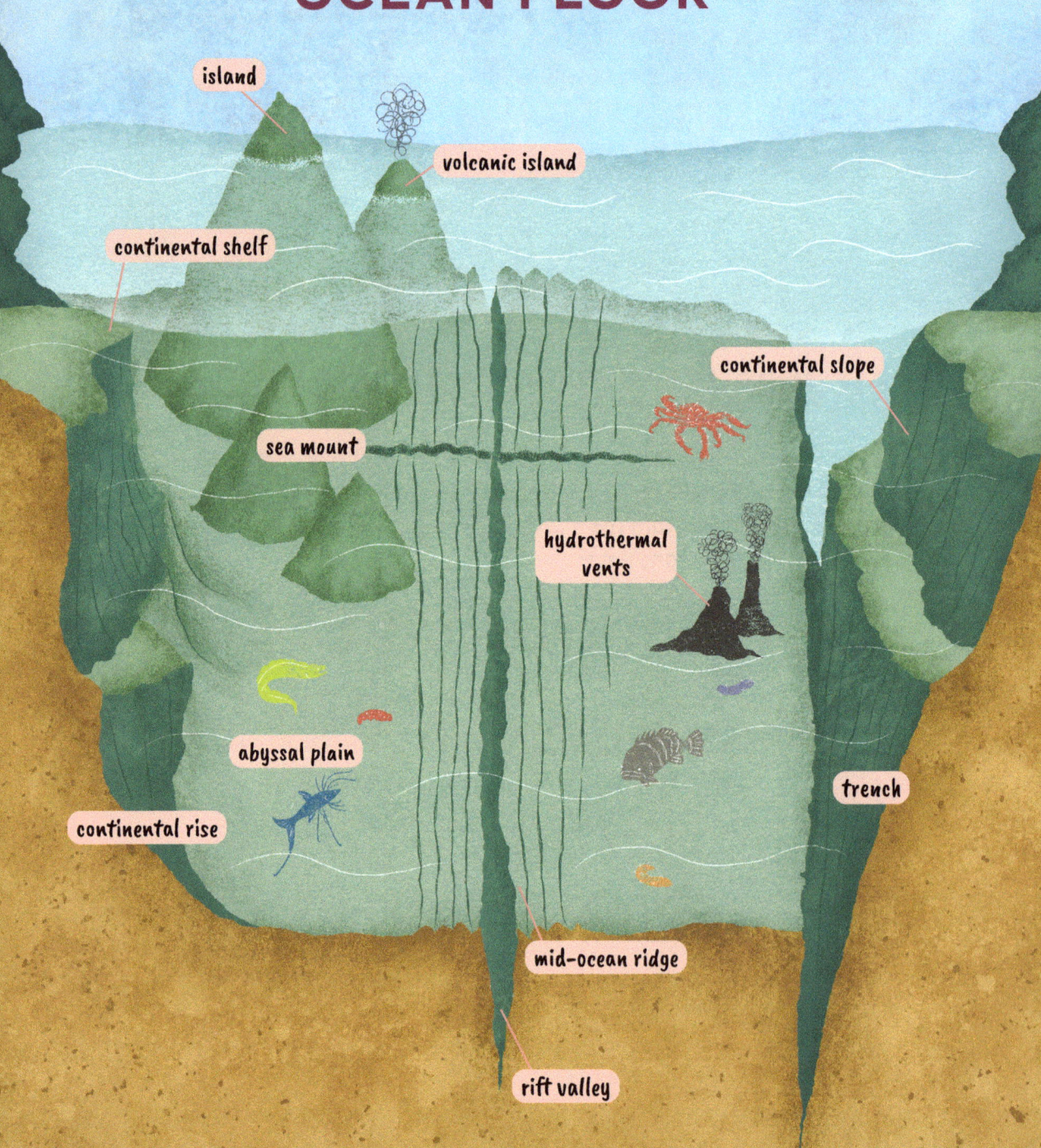

- island
- volcanic island
- continental shelf
- continental slope
- sea mount
- hydrothermal vents
- abyssal plain
- continental rise
- trench
- mid-ocean ridge
- rift valley

DEEP SEA

Imagine a very cold, completely dark place with miles of water overhead. This is the environment of the deep sea, located about 3,280 feet below the surface of the ocean. As you descend into the twilight zone, the light disappears quickly, and by the time you've reached the midnight zone, the average temperature of the water is about 39 degrees Fahrenheit (4°C). The pressure increases the deeper you go. At 3,280 feet below the surface, the pressure is about 100 times greater than that at the surface. Down in the Mariana Trench, the pressure is more than 1,000 times greater! That force is like an adult elephant placing all its weight on just one square inch of seafloor. In this chapter, you will explore other organisms that live here, too, and the ways they survive these intense conditions.

LESSON

ANATOMY OF THE OCEAN FLOOR

The average depth of the ocean is 12,100 feet (3,688 m), more than two miles (3.2 km). Much of the seafloor consists of a layer of *detritus*, or decaying material and sediment. This layer, which in some places can be miles thick, provides a habitat for bottom-dwelling organisms. Food is scarce in these regions, so many organisms that live here scavenge for their food or wait patiently for food to pass by. The Johnson's sea cucumber, a relative of the starfish, slowly crawls through this detritus in search of its meals. Other invertebrates, such as cold-water corals, make their homes here, filterfeeding on particles brought to them by deep currents. The tripod fish has long projections from its fins—like stilts—that can sense food drifting in the currents and then direct the food toward its mouth.

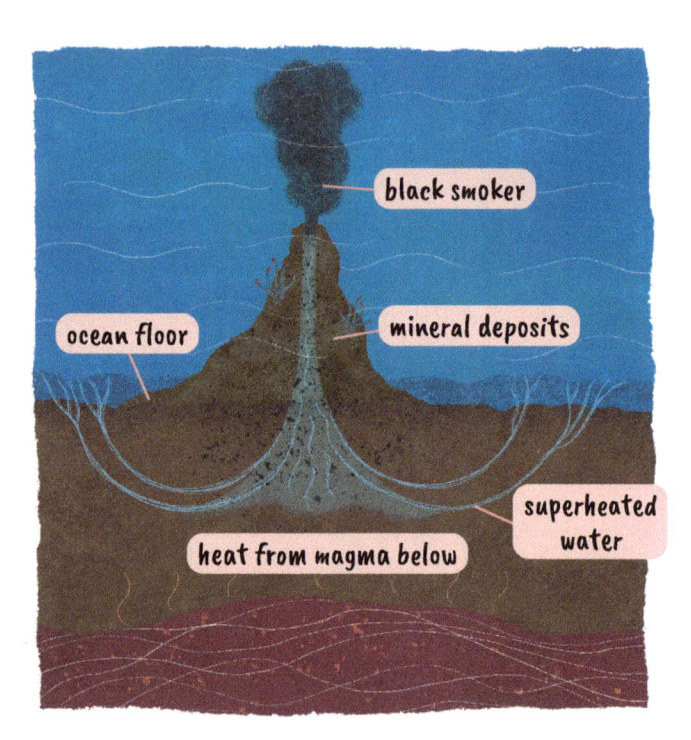

Volcanoes can also be found on the seafloor. Many of these volcanoes are produced in areas where the seafloor is spreading apart. Like volcanoes on land, undersea volcanoes form when *magma*, or molten rock below the crust, pushes through cracks in the Earth's crust. This rock cools to form large undersea mountain ranges, like the Mid-Atlantic Ridge. Water sometimes seeps into these cracks and becomes superheated by the hot magma, sometimes reaching temperatures of 700 degrees Fahrenheit (371°C). Eventually, it bubbles back to the seafloor surface through chimney-like structures call *hydrothermal vents*, a type of hot spring. These vents carry dissolved chemicals from the magma below, such as hydrogen sulfide. Bacteria use hydrogen sulfide to grow using a process called *chemosynthesis*, similar to the way that algae at the surface use the Sun's energy with photosynthesis. This bacteria growth supports a whole ecosystem of other organisms that live near these steaming hot vents, such as vent mussels, a relative of clams and oysters. Pompeii worms, currently known as the most heat-tolerant animal in the world, attach themselves directly to the vent chimneys. They have been known to thrive in temperatures of up to 176 degrees Fahrenheit (80°C)!

Many animals have a symbiotic relationship with the hydrogen sulfide–eating bacteria. The giant tube worm, an invertebrate with no digestive system, grows these bacteria inside their bodies in exchange for the nutrients they create. The Yeti crab grows its own colony of bacteria on its hairy front legs and claws for food.

Fun Fact

Even though the water coming from hydrothermal vents is incredibly hot, it does not boil due to the extreme pressures found on the seafloor.

ACTIVITY

HYDROTHERMAL VENT MODEL

WAIT TIME: 1 DAY

ACTIVITY TIME: 10 TO 20 MINUTES

CATEGORY: INDOOR, MODEL

MATERIALS
8-OUNCE EMPTY WATER BOTTLE
1 POUND OF AIR-DRY CLAY
9-BY-13-INCH SHALLOW BAKING DISH
1 TABLESPOON OF BAKING SODA
SMALL DISH
BLUE FOOD COLORING
SMALL FUNNEL
¼ CUP OF VINEGAR

TIP:
➤ Be sure to quickly remove the funnel to allow you to observe the solution reemerge through the top of your model.

In this activity you are headed to the site of an undersea volcano. You will model the way that hydrothermal vents create hot springs of chemical-rich water on the seafloor. Ocean water seeps through cracks in the seafloor, reaching hot magma. As the water is heated, it dissolves chemicals from the surroundings, carrying it back up with it through the vents.

PREP WORK

Let's begin by creating the hydrothermal vent. Starting from the bottom of the bottle, cover the bottle in air-dry clay. Leave the top of the bottle open. This creates the hydrothermal vent "chimney" that water is released through. Allow it to dry overnight.

STEP-BY-STEP INSTRUCTIONS

1. After your hydrothermal vent is dry and ready for use, place your vent model in a shallow 9-by-13 dish.

2. Put the baking soda in a small dish and add two drops of blue food coloring. The baking soda represents the chemicals found in the Earth's crust and the blue coloring will represent hydrogen sulfide below the vent.

3. Once fully mixed, put the blue baking soda into the hydrothermal vent model through the top opening.

OCEAN ANATOMY ACTIVITIES FOR KIDS

4. Place the funnel through the opening in the top of your model. Pour the vinegar through the funnel. The vinegar represents ocean water seeping through the Earth's crust to reach the hot magma below. What happened? How did the vinegar change after entering the vent? Describe your observations in your journal.

OCEAN JOURNAL ENTRY

In this activity you created a model of a hydrothermal vent. Reflect on your experience to help you answer the questions below.

1. *How is the growth of bacteria around the hydrothermal vent ecosystem similar to the growth of algae within the sunlit ecosystem? How are they different?*

2. *What are some ways in which marine organisms are adapted to living in a hydrothermal vent habitat?*

CONCLUSION:

Hydrothermal vents are hot springs of water with dissolved chemicals found at the bottom of the ocean. They consist of superheated ocean water bubbling up from under the seafloor, where it interacts with magma. You created a model of this process using the chemical reaction between baking soda and vinegar. Just as water seeps through the cracks of the seafloor and reacts with the hot magma, the vinegar in your model vent reacted with the baking soda stored below. Both reactions carry new chemicals from interactions below the surface, before they return up through the vents.

DEEP SEA

LESSON

COUNTERSHADING SQUID

Squid belong to a group of mollusks called *cephalopods*, animals that have tentacles near their heads and swim with jet propulsion. Squid have elongated bodies with eight arms and two longer tentacles, each covered with suckers. The giant squid lives in the twilight zone of the ocean at depths between 1,000 and 2,000 feet. They have large eyes to help them find food in dark waters and can move up to 25 miles per hour (40 kph) when attacking prey. However, they are not at the top of the food chain in this environment. Sperm whales will dive deep in search of giant squid for a meal.

Most squid species live in the open ocean waters searching for fish and shrimp. Unlike some of their mollusk relatives, squid do not have a protective

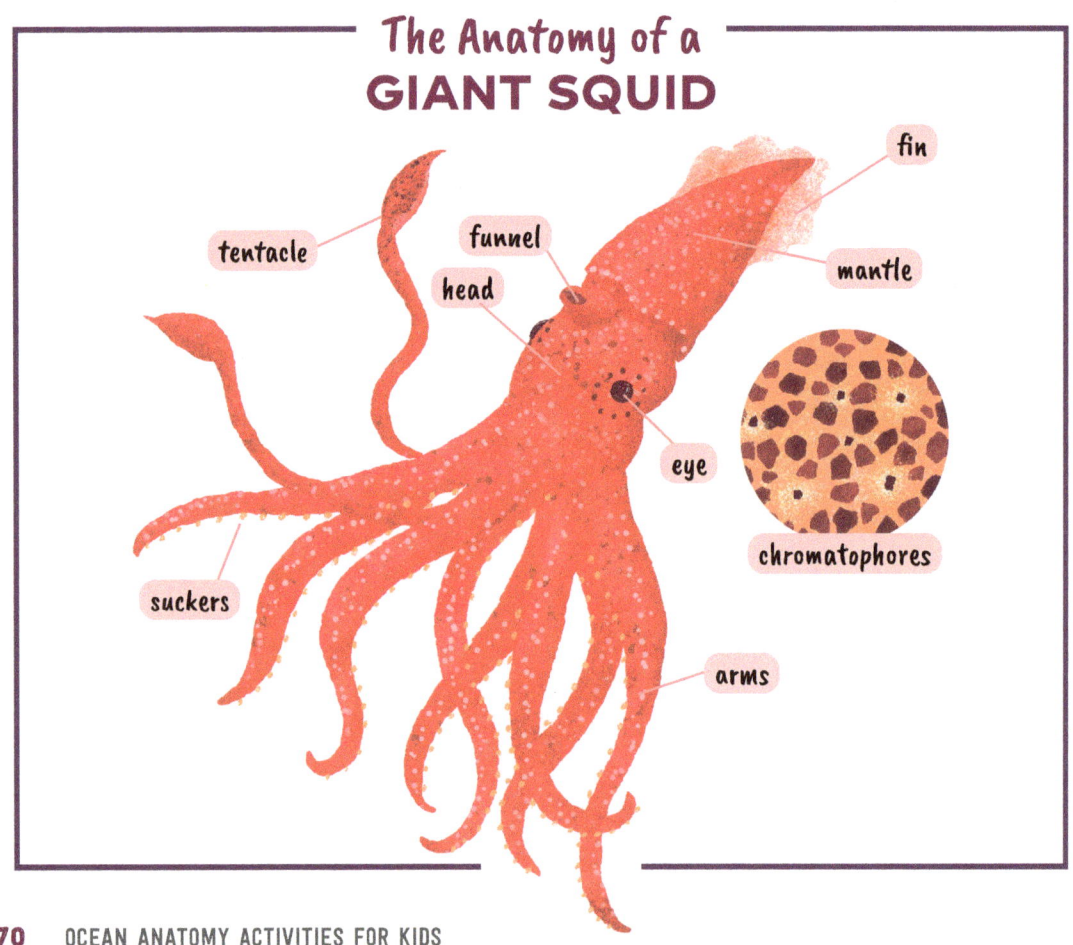

The Anatomy of a GIANT SQUID

tentacle · funnel · head · fin · mantle · eye · chromatophores · suckers · arms

LESSON

shell. Instead, they use camouflage to protect themselves from predators. One form of camouflage used by squid is called *countershading*, in which an animal's coloring is darker on the upper side of their bodies and lighter on the underside. When a predator looks down in search of a squid from above, the darker coloring of the squid's topside blends in with the dark bottom of the ocean, helping it hide. When a predator is searching for a squid from below, the squid's lighter bottom half blends in with the brightly lit ocean surface.

Countershading is not the only camouflage trick used by squid. Their skin contains color-changing organs call *chromatophores*, sac-like organs containing pigments, a type of coloring, that can be black, brown, orange, red, or yellow. The squid can expand and contract these sacs with special muscles. By changing the size of these colored organs, the squid can change its overall coloring to match its surroundings within seconds.

Have you ever noticed how sunlight dances and sparkles in the water? Squid also can mimic the way light changes as it moves through water with special chromatophore organs called *iridophores*, which contain reflective plates that give the squid an iridescent appearance.

Fun Fact

The colossal squid is the heaviest invertebrate animal in the world, with some weighing in at more than 1,000 pounds (453.6 kg).

DEEP SEA 71

ACTIVITY

SQUID CAMOUFLAGE WINDSOCK

WAIT TIME:
30 MINUTES

ACTIVITY TIME:
10 TO 20 MINUTES

CATEGORY:
INDOOR, MODEL

MATERIALS
3 TO 4 SHEETS OF WHITE 8.5-BY-11 CARDSTOCK

MULTIPLE COLORS OF TISSUE PAPER (BLUE, GREEN, YELLOW, AND BROWN)

ALUMINUM FOIL

PAINTBRUSH

CLEAR-DRYING WASHABLE GLUE

STAPLER

MARKERS

SCISSORS

RULER

STRING OR YARN

TIP:
→ If you do not have a stapler, your squid body can be assembled using clear tape.

In this activity, you will create a squid model that shows how it camouflages itself in the open ocean. When choosing colors for your squid model, imagine the squid's environment. Near the surface, ocean filters sparkling sunlight; however, below the squid, you'll find that the deep ocean presents a dark backdrop.

PREP WORK

1. Begin by creating the body of your squid. Squid have long torpedo-shaped bodies. Roll a sheet of the 8.5-by-11 cardstock into a tube and staple in place.

2. Cut eight 2-by-8-inch strips of any color tissue paper. These will represent the arms of the squid.

3. Cut two 2-by-10-inch strips of any color tissue paper. These will represent the tentacles of the squid, which are longer than its arms.

4. Tear small pieces of tissue paper of different colors and sizes to represent the chromatophores that squid use for camouflage. Tear small pieces of aluminum foil of different sizes to represent iridophores.

STEP-BY-STEP INSTRUCTIONS

1. Use the paintbrush to apply glue to the body of your squid. Place most of the small pieces of tissue paper and aluminum foil over the "top" of the squid body. Place only a few on the sides and almost none on the "bottom." Allow the glue to dry. How do the chromatophores of your squid model create countershading? Describe your observations in your journal.

OCEAN ANATOMY ACTIVITIES FOR KIDS

2. Once the glue has dried, it's time to add more details. Staple the arms and tentacles around the bottom of the cylinder. Using markers, draw eyes on your squid body, near the tentacles.

3. Squid have triangular-shaped fins at the back of their bodies opposite their head and tentacles. Using scissors and a ruler, measure and cut a triangle with 8-inch sides from a piece of white cardstock. Staple or glue this to the top side of your squid, allowing the corners to reach out past the squid body.

4. Finally, make a small hole on each side of your squid model near the top, on the opposite end of the tentacles. Tie one end of the string to one of the holes and tie the other end to the other hold to create a loop. This will let you hang your squid outside in a light breeze.

5. Watch your squid capture the wind. Imagine it is swimming near the surface of the ocean. What do you notice about how the sunlight affects your squid's appearance? Record your observations in your journal.

OCEAN JOURNAL ENTRY

Answer the questions below in your journal.

1. *Describe how chromatophores and iridophores are used by squid to create camouflage.*

2. *In what ways is your squid model similar to or different from a squid in camouflage?*

CONCLUSION:
In this activity you created a windsock model of a squid. When your model blows in the breeze it simulates squid camouflage. When decorating your squid's body you used tissue paper to represent chromatophores and aluminum foil to represent iridophores. Adding more of these organs to the top of your squid simulates the countershading effect seen in squid found in the open ocean. The movement of the windsock model through the breeze simulates the way iridophores reflect light from the surface of a squid's skin while swimming in the ocean.

DEEP SEA

LESSON

BIOLUMINESCENCE

Many of the animal species that live in the deep ocean have adapted to living in constant darkness with the ability to create their own light, called *bioluminescence*. Bioluminescence is a chemical process that generates light within living organisms. If you have ever seen a firefly light up at dusk, then you have witnessed bioluminescence. Scientists estimate that 76 percent of known marine animals create bioluminescence!

Organisms that produce bioluminescence contain a chemical called *luciferin* within their bodies. When the animal combines luciferin with oxygen, light is created. This is similar to breaking a glow stick: Liquids mix within the tube to create a light-generating chemical reaction.

Marine organisms create light for several reasons. In many cases, bioluminescence helps predators attract prey. Deep-sea anglerfish have a bioluminescent lure attached to their head. It dangles the lure in front of its large mouth in hopes of drawing prey close enough for a quick bite. Some animals use bioluminescence to attract mates instead of prey. The female syllid fireworm, found on the seafloor, signals mates with bright flashes.

Some animals use bioluminescence to find their food. The stoplight loosejaw fish has the ability to produce two colors of light—both green and red. Red light is completely gone from the midnight zone these fish inhabit, so the stoplight loosejaw's prey is not adapted to seeing it. Using red light, the loosejaw can see its prey without the prey seeing it back.

Other animals use bioluminescence to startle or distract predators. Instead of squirting dark ink as a distraction, like the squid species living in the sunlight zones, the vampire squid found in the twilight zone lets out a substance filled with bioluminescent particles that can glow with twinkling light for up to 10 minutes, confusing the predator.

Fun Fact

While 76 percent of known marine organisms create bioluminescence, it is very rare in freshwater organisms.

ACTIVITY

FISHING LIKE AN ANGLERFISH

WAIT TIME:
1 HOUR

TIME:
20 TO 30 MINUTES

CATEGORY:
INDOOR, CRAFT

MATERIALS
NEWSPAPER
2 PAPER PLATES
WASHABLE PAINT (DARK BLUE, BLACK, OR RED)
2-INCH CIRCLE OF WHITE CARDSTOCK
GLOW-IN-THE-DARK PAINT
SCISSORS
TOOTHPICKS
STAPLER
GLUE OR TAPE
MARKERS
HOLE PUNCH
PIPE CLEANER

In this activity, you have a chance to simulate how organisms in the deep sea use light to lure prey in close. Using your imagination and creativity you will create an anglerfish model, complete with a glow-in-the-dark lure. Once it's complete, observe how the lure works to attract prey.

Safety First! *Toothpicks can be very sharp, so handle them with care to avoid injury.*

PREP WORK

1. Lay down some newspaper or other covering to protect your workspace. Turn both paper plates upside down. Paint the entire bottom of both plates with dark paint. Most species of anglerfish are not brightly colored since most animals do not have to see well in deep ocean zones. Allow the plates to dry completely. These will become the body of your fish.

2. Paint one side of the cardstock circle with the glow-in-the-dark paint, allowing it to dry before painting the other side. This will create the bioluminescent lure for your fish.

3. Stack both painted paper plates one on top of the other. Using scissors, cut out a large triangular-shaped piece from the stack, like a piece of pie. You should end up with two triangle pieces that are about a quarter of the size of the original paper plates.

DEEP SEA 75

ACTIVITY

4. Cut one of the triangles in half. These will become the two pectoral fins on the side of the body of your anglerfish.

5. Fold the other triangle piece in half. This will become the tail fin of your anglerfish. The leftover paper plates will form the body.

STEP-BY-STEP INSTRUCTIONS

1. Species of anglerfish often have extremely large mouths with very long, sharp, pointy teeth. The toothpicks will represent these teeth. On the unpainted sides of both plates, tape the toothpicks around the opening you cut out the triangle from. These will be your anglerfish's mouth.

2. Now it's time to attach the tail. On one paper plate, on the opposite side of the mouth, glue half of the folded triangle to the unpainted side, allowing the rest to hang off the plate.

3. Once the teeth and tail have been attached, place the unpainted sides of the plates together, making sure to match up both sides of the mouth. Staple the plates together along the edge to create the final fish body.

4. Next, glue or tape the pectoral fins to the fish body, one on each side.

5. Using markers, draw small dark eyes near the top of the mouth. Anglerfish do not have large eyes or great eyesight.

6. It's time to add the anglerfish's lure. Using a hole punch, make a hole through the glow-in-the-dark circle. Attach one end of the pipe cleaner through the hole. Cut a hole in your fish body near the top of the mouth and attach the other end of the pipe cleaner. Many

TIP:

➡ If you would like to have a three-dimensional lure you can substitute the paper circle for a glow-in-the-dark bead.

76 OCEAN ANATOMY ACTIVITIES FOR KIDS

anglerfish species dangle the glowing end of their lure next to their large mouths.

7. Place the lure under direct light for 5 minutes. This acts to "charge" the paint of the lure. Imagine this is like the mixing of chemicals inside the lure.

8. Enter a dark room and observe the light given off from the lure. Move the lure back and forth. What does it look like? Write your observations in your journal.

CONCLUSION:
In this lesson, you created your own version of an anglerfish. These fish use a bioluminescent lure attached to their head. They dangle it in front of their mouth to lure prey closer. You created an example of this behavior when you moved your crafted fish in a dark space.

OCEAN JOURNAL ENTRY

In this activity you crafted a model of an anglerfish, complete with a bioluminescent lure used to attract prey. Use your experience to answer the following questions in your journal.

1. *Describe at least two ways deep-sea marine life use bioluminescence.*

2. *To power the light from your anglerfish lure, you needed to expose it to light for some time. How does a real anglerfish create bioluminescence?*

3. *Imagine having your own built-in flashlight! In what ways would this be useful to you?*

The Arctic Region

- polar bear
- snowy owl
- arctic fox
- arctic hare
- walrus
- narwhals

The Antarctic Region

- orca
- emperor penguin
- Adélie penguin
- Weddell seal

POLAR REGIONS

This chapter takes you on an expedition to the polar regions: the Arctic Ocean in the north and the continent of Antarctica in the south. These polar regions contain the coldest climates on the planet: The coldest temperature ever recorded was in Antarctica at -128.6 degrees Fahrenheit (-89.2°C) in 1983. Much of the land and sea at the poles is covered by snow and ice throughout the year, and winter lasts from March until October. The Arctic Ocean is the smallest ocean on Earth and covers about 3 percent of the Earth's surface. It is home to marine mammals like the polar bear, walrus, and narwhal. The continent of Antarctica holds almost 90 percent of all the world's ice and 70 percent of the world's freshwater—locked in ice. Here you will see animals such as the emperor penguin, Weddell seals, and orcas.

LESSON

SEA ICE

The formation of *sea ice*, or frozen ocean water that forms in the polar regions, is incredibly important, not only to the polar ecosystems but also to the global climate. In the arctic, sea ice forms over the Arctic Ocean. In the Antarctic, sea ice forms around the continent of Antarctica. These polar ice sheets, which range in thickness from mere inches up to 15 feet (4.5 m), grow during cold winter months. They get smaller in the summer but do not completely disappear.

Sea ice can't hold much salt. When it forms, most of the salt is concentrated into the ocean water below the ice. This incredibly salty water is denser than the surrounding seawater and therefore sinks toward the seafloor. This sinking creates a current of cool water toward the equator, helping moderate the world's climate.

ice sheet

sea ice

land

sea

seafloor

OCEAN ANATOMY ACTIVITIES FOR KIDS

While the formation of sea ice creates temperature-regulating currents, the amount of sea ice is important to maintaining global climate as well. You may have noticed on a warm sunny day that wearing dark-colored clothing can make you feel incredibly hot. The color of surfaces affects how much of the Sun's energy is reflected from it. Darker colors absorb more heat energy than lighter colored materials do.

While this phenomenon affects how much heat is absorbed by your clothing, it is also true for the surface of the Earth. Bright-white sea ice reflects sunlight and keeps the polar regions cool. Up to 80 percent of the sunlight hitting the surface of the ice is reflected into space. When the sunlight strikes the surface of the dark-colored ocean, 90 percent of the Sun's light is absorbed. Warming temperatures gradually melt sea ice over time, reducing the amount of reflective surface and increasing the amount of heat absorption. About 15 percent of the world's oceans are covered by sea ice during part of the year. A steady reduction of this coverage contributes to global warming.

Fun Fact

Polar bears are the largest land carnivores in the world, and they use sea ice to hunt for seals.

ACTIVITY

KEEPING COOL WITH SEA ICE

TIME:
10 TO 20 MINUTES

CATEGORY:
INDOOR OR OUTDOOR, EXPERIMENT

MATERIALS
1 (8.5-BY-11) SHEET OF BLACK CONSTRUCTION PAPER

STAPLER

1 (8.5-BY-11) SHEET OF WHITE CONSTRUCTION PAPER

TWO THERMOMETERS

A WARM, SUNNY DAY

TIP:

→ Try this inside using a 60-watt incandescent light bulb or reptile heat lamp. Hold the pockets 8 inches away from the lamp. Try once using a lamp and once using only the outdoor sunshine. Do you notice a difference between each experiment?

Does the color of a surface really affect the absorption of the Sun's heat energy? The polar ice caps are extremely bright compared to the color of the dark ocean waters that they cover. How do they affect the local climate? In this activity, you will explore the answers to these questions.

Safety First!
- Use caution when handling glass incandescent bulbs or reptile heat lamps to avoid breakage.
- Incandescent bulbs and reptile heat lamps can become extremely hot. Be sure not to touch the bulb after it has been lit.

PREP WORK

Fold the black sheet of construction paper in half lengthwise. Staple the folded sides together to create a pocket with an opening on top. Do the same thing with the white paper.

STEP-BY-STEP INSTRUCTIONS

1. Create a table with two columns in your journal. Label one column "white" and the other column "black." On the first row of each column record the starting temperature readings of both thermometers. The white construction paper envelope represents the arctic ice sheets over the poles. The black envelope represents exposed ocean waters once the ice sheets recede.

2. Place one thermometer tip in each construction paper pocket. Put both pockets outside in a sunny spot. In your journal, write a hypothesis about how you think the temperature will change after both pockets are exposed to the light.

3. Record temperatures of each thermometer in your table every 2 minutes for 10 minutes. How did the temperatures change over time? How are the temperatures similar or different between the two different colored envelopes? Do your observations support your hypothesis?

OCEAN JOURNAL ENTRY

This activity studied the effects of surface color on heat absorption. Reflect on your observations as you answer the following questions in your journal.

1. *How do you think the loss of sea ice would affect temperature in the polar regions?*

2. *If sea ice formation was reduced, how might that affect deep water currents traveling from the poles?*

CONCLUSION:

In this lesson you headed to the poles to observe the sea ice and its effects on the global temperature. The formation of sea ice plays an important role in keeping the Earth cool. The white-colored surface of sea ice reflects a large amount of the Sun's heat energy. This can be observed by the change in temperatures in your experiment. A white-colored surface like the pocket in your experiment stays cooler than the dark-colored pocket. Light energy is reflected by the white paper and absorbed by the black paper.

POLAR REGIONS 83

LESSON

GLACIERS AND ICEBERGS

Glaciers and icebergs are different from sea ice because they are formed on land out of compressed freshwater rain and snow. Eventually this compression forces snow to re-form into large ice crystals. This process can take hundreds of years and form ice crystals as big as baseballs! In Antarctica, glaciers can be up to 3 miles (1.6 km) deep. Over millions of years, the large amounts of packed ice in glaciers create depressions and carve valleys in the land below. The Great Lakes in North America are believed to have formed during a period in the Earth's history when glaciers extended from the North Pole down to where the United States is today. Melted freshwater from glaciers collects in low areas to form shallow pools on the glacial surface called *lakes*. The narrow channels that carry this water through the glacier to its base are called *moulins*. As a glacier moves from growth or melting, large, deep cracks called *crevasses* can form in the ice.

snow cover

lakes

glacier flow

crevasses

ice

moulins

icebergs

84 OCEAN ANATOMY ACTIVITIES FOR KIDS

LESSON

Icebergs are large chunks of glaciers that have broken off into the sea, a process known as calving. The world's largest recorded iceberg, B-15, broke off of the Ross Ice Shelf in Antarctica in March 2000. It measured more than 4,000 square miles (6,437 km^2). Sometimes air is pushed out of the ice crystals when it is compressed as a glacier. Icebergs that break off from these glaciers have few to no air bubbles, making them appear crystalline and transparent.

Only 10 percent of an iceberg is seen above water, leaving the majority hidden below sea level. This phenomenon gave rise to the phrase "the tip of the iceberg," referring to the unknown factors of a circumstance. The hidden ice below the surface of an iceberg can pose a danger for ships traveling among them. Sharp, jagged ice can tear holes in the bottom of the vessel. This is what happened in 1912, when the *Titanic* struck an iceberg and sank. Following the tragedy, an international iceberg patrol was established to keep track of dangerous icebergs traveling in the path of ocean liners.

Fun Fact

Bergy seltzer is the term that mariners use to describe the fizzing sound icebergs make as they melt. The sound comes from the gradual release of air bubbles trapped within the ice.

ACTIVITY

MELTING ICEBERGS

TIME:
10 TO 20 MINUTES

CATEGORY:
INDOOR, MODEL

MATERIALS
2 SMALL BOWLS
½ CUP OF VEGETABLE OIL
BLUE FOOD COLORING
2 CUPS OF WATER
FUNNEL
EMPTY WATER BOTTLE WITH A CAP
SPOON FOR MIXING

TIP:

→ Try freezing some of the oil mixture in an ice cube tray. Place a finished ice cube on top of the oil layer. Imagine that this is an iceberg. What do you notice about its position in the mixture? Write your observations in your journal.

What happens to the water of an iceberg after it melts? In this activity you will examine how ocean water ends up layered due to the density differences between iceberg meltwater and salty ocean water.

PREP WORK

1. In a small bowl, mix together the vegetable oil and 1 drop of blue food coloring. This will represent meltwater from icebergs, created as they float into warmer waters.

2. In a separate bowl, mix together the water and 3 drops of blue food coloring.

STEP-BY-STEP INSTRUCTIONS

1. Imagine the darker blue water is cold, salty seawater found at the North and South poles. This water is denser than freshwater, so it sinks to the bottom of the ocean. Using a funnel, pour the blue water into the bottom of the plastic bottle.

2. Next, using the funnel, add the oil mixture to your bottle. This represents the freshwater that melts from icebergs. Just like sea ice, icebergs cannot hold salt and are therefore less dense than salty seawater. What happens to the solution in the bottle after this layer is added? Write your observations in your journal.

OCEAN ANATOMY ACTIVITIES FOR KIDS

3. Put the cap tightly on the bottle. Gently shake the bottle. What happens to the mixture? Allow the bottle to sit undisturbed for 10 minutes. How does your mixture change over time? Record your observations in your journal.

CONCLUSION:

In this activity, you created a model of an ocean water column to demonstrate what happens as icebergs melt when they float into warmer waters. Cold, salty seawater has a greater density than the fresh meltwater of icebergs. Therefore, iceberg meltwater tends to float near the surface after it melts. You observed this phenomenon when the oil mixture floated above the water mixture in the bottle.

OCEAN JOURNAL ENTRY

This activity provided you with an opportunity to observe the density-dependent layering of ocean water that occurs when icebergs melt. Reflect on your experience as you answer the questions below in your journal.

1. *Describe how icebergs form. How do they disappear?*

2. *How is glacier formation different from sea ice formation? How is it the same?*

POLAR REGIONS

LESSON

HOW ANIMALS KEEP WARM

If you are cold, you might choose to put on a sweater or coat. This extra clothing traps our body heat to keep us warm. Since humans are mammals, and all mammals are warm-blooded, we must maintain a specific internal body temperature to survive. In this lesson we will learn how marine mammals of the polar regions, such as whales, seals, sea lions, and polar bears, have unique ways to keep warm in their extremely cold environment.

For many water-dwelling marine mammals, large amounts of fur can slow down their swimming, making it more difficult to catch fish. Instead, marine mammals have evolved an internal system of insulation in the form of a thick layer of *blubber*. Blubber is a type of fat beneath the skin that helps animals store energy, keep warm, and increase buoyancy, making it easier to float.

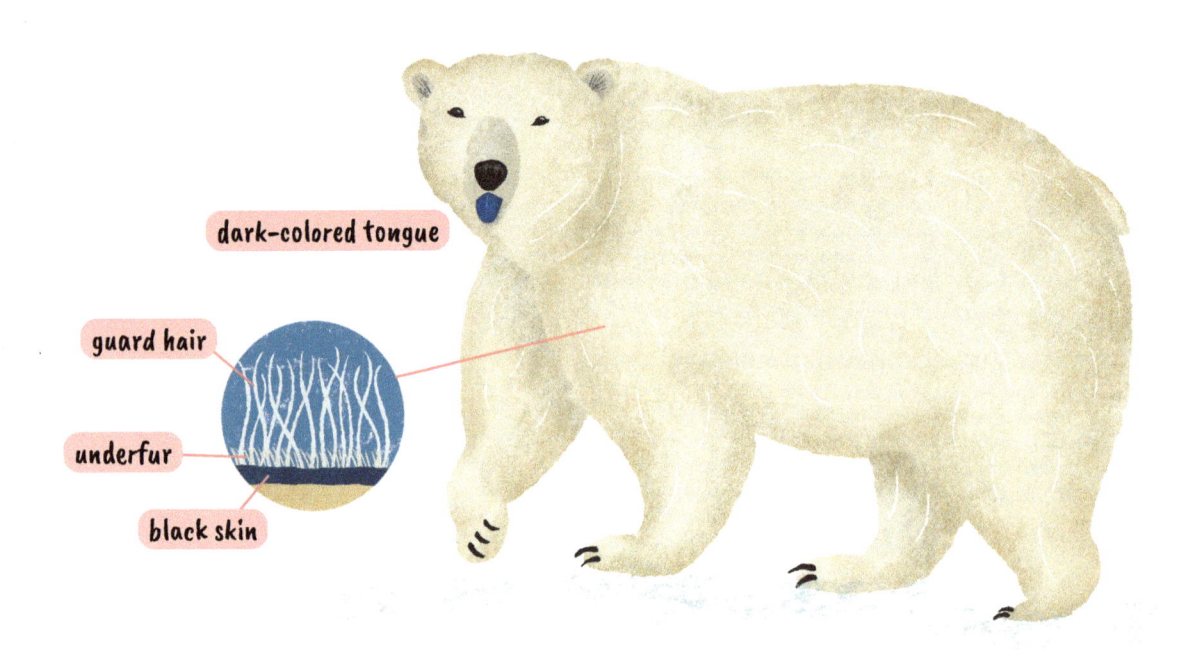

- dark-colored tongue
- guard hair
- underfur
- black skin

88 OCEAN ANATOMY ACTIVITIES FOR KIDS

LESSON

Sometimes called "unicorns of the sea," narwhals are a type of toothed whale that live in the Arctic Ocean. Males often have a large, straight horn coming from their heads. This horn is in fact a tusk, like that of a walrus or an elephant. In the narwhal this tusk forms from the left front tooth of the whale. Narwhals spend their time fishing between sea ice sheets. To withstand the constant cold temperatures of their environment, a narwhal's body can be up to 40 percent blubber.

A polar bear's adaptations to staying warm combine both fur and blubber. In addition to a four-inch layer of blubber underneath their skin, a polar bear has two layers of fur. A short, dense underlayer is covered by a longer layer of protection called *guard hairs*. A polar bear's fur appears white but is actually transparent and hollow like a straw. The hollow structure of the fur reflects light, making it appear white. This white appearance has a bonus for the bear. It provides camouflage in the snow and ice, helping polar bears sneak up on their prey.

Fun Fact

Harp seals can weigh up to 300 pounds (136 kg) with all of their blubber, but before they get that big, they have long white fur to keep them warm.

ACTIVITY

MARINE MAMMAL INSULATION

TIME:
10 TO 15 MINUTES

CATEGORY:
INDOOR, EXPERIMENT

MATERIALS
1 CUP OF VEGETABLE SHORTENING
TWO RUBBER GLOVES
5-GALLON BUCKET OF ICE WATER
STOPWATCH

How do polar bears and other marine mammals manage to swim for long periods of time in icy arctic waters? In this activity you will test the insulation abilities of vegetable shortening, a type of fat. How long will this type of insulation keep you feeling warm? Complete the activity below to find out.

PREP WORK

1. Gather your materials to work in an area that you don't mind getting wet.

2. Put the vegetable shortening inside one rubber glove.

STEP-BY-STEP INSTRUCTIONS

1. Put one hand inside the rubber glove with vegetable shortening. Be sure to spread shortening evenly throughout the inside of the glove. The shortening is a type of fat, like blubber. Imagine your hand is a narwhal equipped with a thick layer of blubber to insulate against the cold.

2. Fit the other glove over your other hand. This hand will represent a human without the thick layer of blubber that the narwhal has.

3. Place both glove-covered hands into the bucket of ice water. Do you notice a difference in the temperature you feel in each hand? Time how long you can hold each hand in the ice-water bucket. Which gloved hand stays warmer longer? Write your observations in your journal.

TIP:

→ Have someone else try the experiment. Compare and contrast their results with your results. How are they the same or different?

4. Find other materials that you think might help to keep the uninsulated hand warm, such as cotton balls or shredded newspapers. Add these to the plain glove. Repeat the experiment. Did your results change? If so, how?

CONCLUSION:

Some animals, like the polar bear, use multiple layers of fur and a thick layer of blubber to insulate their bodies against the cold. In this experiment, vegetable shortening was used in place of blubber. By comparing the feeling of ice water on your hands, with and without the fatty insulation, you were able to experience how well blubber keeps polar animals warm.

OCEAN JOURNAL ENTRY

In this activity you explored how blubber is used by marine mammals to stay warm. Reflect on your experience from the activity to help you answer the questions below.

1. *Which material seemed to insulate against the ice water the best? Why do you think this?*

2. *What advantage do polar bears have by having both fur and blubber? Why would having fur be a disadvantage for a narwhal?*

RESOURCES

Use these resources to expand your exploration of marine science topics. The videos and books provide detailed explanations on specific topics in marine science. The websites provide digital resources and curricula with additional learning activities that complement this book. The organizations provide easily navigable fact-based resources for additional learning.

BOOKS

Jacques Cousteau: The Ocean World by Jacques-Yves Cousteau

Oceanology: The Secrets of the Sea Revealed by Maya Plass

WEBSITES

SEA Curriculum from the University of Hawaii at Manoa: Manoa.Hawaii.edu/sealearning

Lawrence Hall of Science: Mare.LawrenceHallOfScience.org

Marine Science Explorers: MarineScienceExplorers.com/resources

ORGANIZATIONS

National Oceanographic and Atmospheric Administration: OceanService.NOAA.gov/kids

National Geographic Ocean Education: NationalGeographic.org/education

VIDEOS

"How Do Ocean Currents Work?" TEDEd by Jennifer Verduin: Ed.TED.com/lessons/how-do-ocean-currents-work-jennifer-verduin

ACKNOWLEDGMENTS

I'd like to thank my husband, Eric, for supporting all of my educational and professional endeavors. There is no better partner for sharing my love of exploring our ocean planet. I'd like to thank my parents for always encouraging me to pursue my dreams. And lastly, I'd like to devote a special thank-you to all of my previous science educators for instilling in me a lifelong passion for learning.

ABOUT THE AUTHOR

Laura Petrusic is a professionally certified science teacher and marine science educator. She holds an undergraduate degree in marine science from the University of South Carolina and a master's degree in science education from the Florida Institute of Technology. Laura has designed and delivered marine science educational content to students of all ages, creating programs within the formal classroom, outdoor education, science centers, and homeschool groups.

She is the curriculum and content developer for Marine Science Explorers and offers a variety of online courses for K–12 students in marine science. Her philosophy of learning is inquiry based, integrated, and student centered, thus allowing students to make connections with the natural world in a way that is relative to their lives.

Laura currently lives in Lake Mary, Florida. When she is not teaching, she enjoys beachcombing and camping adventures with her husband and three children.